A

MODERN
PROPHET

Answers Your Key
Questions about Life

Also by Harold Klemp

MAHANTA

This book has been authored by and published under
the supervision of the Mahanta, the Living ECK Master,
Sri Harold Klemp. It is the Word of ECK.

A

MODERN
PROPHET

Answers Your Key
Questions about Life

Book 2

HAROLD KLEMP

ECKANKAR
Minneapolis
www.Eckankar.org

A Modern Prophet Answers Your Key Questions about Life, Book 2

Copyright © 2010 ECKANKAR

Printed in USA
Compiled by Mary Carroll Moore
Edited by Patrick Carroll, Joan Klemp, and Anthony Moore
Text illustrations by Rebecca Lorio
Back cover photo by Robert Huntley

Library of Congress Cataloging-in-Publication Data

Klemp, Harold.
    A modern prophet answers your key questions about life / Harold Klemp.
        p. cm.
    ISBN 978-1-57043-307-8 (alk. paper)
    1. Eckankar (Organization)—Miscellanea.   2. Spiritual life—Miscellanea.   I. Title.
BP605.E3K56455   1998
299'.93—dc21   98-24225
                                         CIP

♾ This paper meets the requirements of ANSI/NISO Z39.48-1992 (Permanence of Paper).

Contents

v

ercises • Experiences with the Mahanta • Becoming Self-Reliant • Born into ECK • Rite of Passage • God-Realization • Brothers of the Leaf • Initiation Signposts • What Is the Light and Sound? • Ups and Downs of the True Spiritual Path • Led to the Path • Working Consciously with the Masters • Blue Star of ECK • What's Different about Eckankar? • Path to Mastership

Introduction

$\mathcal{W}$hen you travel the road to God, you venture into uncharted territory. Sometimes a crossroads will appear: Which direction do you take? Decisions made in the smallest parts of your life can affect the success of your journey.

How do you decide? Is there anyone who has been there before and can answer your questions?

The sincere seeker of truth often finds that his real questions go without an answer and his inner experiences with the Light and Sound of God are not explained. Where can he find someone who has already traveled the road to God—and come back to tell about it?

Harold Klemp is one such person. He is a modern-day prophet. As the spiritual leader of Eckankar, he gets thousands of letters from seekers of truth around the world. All want direct and useful answers about how to travel the road to God. Harold replies personally to many of these letters with insights and advice from his own experience.

The teachings of ECK define the nature of Soul. You are Soul, a particle of God sent into the worlds (including earth) to gain spiritual experience.

The goal in ECK is spiritual freedom in this lifetime, after which you become a Co-worker with God, both here and in the next world. Karma and reincarnation are primary beliefs.

Where can the sincere seeker of truth find someone who has already traveled the road to God—and come back to tell about it?

Key to the ECK teachings is the Mahanta, the Living ECK Master. He has the special ability to act as both the Inner and Outer Master for ECK students. The prophet of Eckankar, he is given respect but is not worshipped. He teaches the sacred name of God, HU. When sung just a few minutes each day, HU will lift you spiritually into the Light and Sound of God—the ECK (Holy Spirit). This easy spiritual exercise and others will purify you. You are then able to accept the full love of God in this lifetime.

Sri Harold Klemp is the Mahanta, the Living ECK Master today. Author of many books, discourses, and articles, he teaches the ins and outs of the spiritual life. Many of his talks are available to you on audio and video recordings. His teachings lift people and help them recognize and understand their own experiences in the Light and Sound of God.

In this book are some three hundred questions and answers to help you live a life of joy, service, and contentment.

In this book are some three hundred questions and answers to help you live a life of joy, service, and contentment.

The topics he covers in *A Modern Prophet Answers Your Key Questions about Life*, Book 2, are many. They range from who you are as Soul living in this world to understanding your dreams, past lives, and karmic lessons. They include family and relationships, health and healing, spiritual protection, the ECK Masters, living with divine love, and service to all life.

Ponder upon these topics. You will benefit at every stage of your journey home to God. Now, get set to read and learn more about you.

To find out more about the author and Eckankar, please turn to pages 275–81 in the back of this book.

People in this supersonic world wanted to be reborn into this era.

1
LIVING IN
THIS WORLD

Nowadays most people, at least in the Western world, feel they are in need of more time. They rush around trying to accomplish a lot of things. The pace of life is speeded up, and some feel that time is taking more and more of their attention. Is this fast pace of life made up by mankind, or does it come from somewhere else? What lesson is Soul supposed to get from these experiences?

Life today truly flies at a supersonic speed. Two main viewpoints in regard to this phenomenon exist.

One, people are victims of technology. But its attractions, like the cell phone, to name only one of hundreds, is like candy. It's hard to give up one's need for it. Yet both, in excess, are a health concern—one spiritual, the other physical.

We love our addictions. Otherwise we wouldn't do them.

The second view of today's rat race is less common. In short it says, "We don't have to live like this." So

Life today flies at supersonic speed. What lesson is Soul to get from these experiences?

1

people rearrange their jobs and lifestyles to enter a calmer, more sane existence. Of course, it means the sacrifice of some candies.

Lin Yutang, a modern Chinese wise man, said to let one thing go. Sage advice with many ramifications.

When your schedule gets out of hand, just let one thing go. It can put you in control again.

When your schedule gets out of hand, just let one thing go. In fact, it may take doing more than once in an hour. You'd be surprised how such a simple idea can put you in control of your time again.

Make no mistake, people in this supersonic world wanted to be reborn into this era. Even if they had a choice to come at a more placid time or in a more settled age. Yet complaints are an inborn part of human nature. People like to complain about self-made troubles.

The lesson for Soul is patience and humility. The gadgets are like badges that scream: "Look how important I am!" "Me, top-drawer stuff—compared to you."

What else is that but vanity? So it needs humility.

Catching the Right Wave

I realize some people—including myself at times—want to believe in chance so as to evade personal responsibility. Yet even when we're ready and willing to accept responsibility for our thoughts, words, and deeds, it does seem we still have to "catch the right wave" before we achieve success in our endeavors. Can you shed some light on this?

To "catch the right wave." Fortune has a habit of finding those who can make a plan and stick with it. True, one person out of a million hits the big time by winning the lottery, but don't plan your fortune or future by simply buying lottery tickets week after week.

Winners make their own luck.

Many people who deal with failure have the peculiar habit of self-destruction. For example, a student may study moderately hard nearly the whole school term, yet then neglect to study for the final exam. Or even worse, not show up at all. Why?

The first step to finding success is being true to yourself and others.

Simple English, please?

Do everything, large or small, as if you were doing it for God alone. That means the task will be done with love, joy, and (don't forget) thoroughness.

Success is a little like heaven: There's always another step. A corollary of that idea is that success comes about in steps. And a plan simply creates those steps in the imagination, then on paper, then in reality.

Do every-thing, large or small, as if you were doing it for God alone, with love, joy, and thoroughness.

Life Is a Gift

On this journey home to God, we are sometimes faced with painful experiences. During these times, some people make the choice to end their lives. What is the spiritual lesson and responsibility in making that choice?

Life often is pain. If not physical pain, then surely emotional or mental dis-ease of some sort. Earth is God's boot camp for Souls.

People who take their lives are to be pitied only because they threw away on a whim the divine blessing of this life. In Christianity, it would be a final tragedy. The reason is that its belief system admits but to a single human existence in eternity and to lightly gamble it away is to forever suffer eternal damnation.

The teachings of Eckankar view human life on a broader scale. Each human life *is* a precious gift of God. After all, survival is one of our key teachings. Life is to cherish. Be respectful of all life, especially your own.

Be respectful of all life, especially your own.

When someone commits suicide, it's due to ignorance or a willful disobedience of spiritual law. That person has made a shortsighted choice. The spiritual hierarchy will require that Soul to make amends in another human life, and another, under much more trying conditions. Finally, that Soul learns that suicide is no answer. Just another problem.

Finding the Right Job

In doing what we love and loving what we do, are there jobs that don't help us spiritually? If so, why? And what can we do about it?

If two people love what they do but one is evil and the other is good, what would you expect of each?

At the national level, the first might love being a dictator or tyrant, while the second would be viewed as a wise, bold leader. At the neighborhood level, the evil-hearted one might love being a thief. The other, a doctor. At the family level, the first might like cruelty or argument, while the other opts for peace and reconciliation.

So, a job is a job is a job.

What makes the difference is what lies in an individual's heart.

Life, of course, is not so simple. Is anyone on earth all good or all evil? No, everyone is somewhere in between.

So there may be a Robin Hood whose stolen goods go, in part, to charity. Again, a doctor who gives unnecessary treatments to feed his bank account. Little is black or white, good or evil, pure justice or injustice—due to the influence of karma.

Free will is, therefore, an important element. Yet it rises from an individual's state of consciousness, because past experience whispers advice about the merits or risks of a course of action.

With all the above at play, you do know what jobs are good for you. Follow your heart. Learn the spiritual lessons in any given job. Then move on to a new challenge. So, a job is a job is a job. Your love and attention bring it to life, though, so stay with one— through thick and thin—until you've learned all it can teach you.

Follow your heart. Learn the spiritual lessons in any given job.

Our Spiritual Freedom

In a talk you mentioned we are fortunate to be able to travel worldwide to meet together at seminars and that we may not always have this opportunity in the future. What did you mean, and what would cause such a change in our freedom?

The future depends mainly upon the choices that people make. It is called free will.

A crisis of large proportions does loom for the human race due to the population explosion. Yet there are other pressures too. Some of these are political or geological, but underneath, they merely reflect a widespread misunderstanding about karma.

The idea so many have today is that one can cheat, lie, or steal without any consequences. It's an illusion.

There's no such thing as a free lunch.

The idea so many have today is that one can cheat, lie, or steal without any consequences. It's an illusion.

Negative thoughts, words, and deeds cause the spiritual forces to impose limits upon the exercise of such behavior. As the negative stream is shut down somewhat, to bring harmony into the picture again, the negative forces resist. They, in turn, impose natural or legal restrictions on all outer freedoms.

The idea is of this order: If I can't have more candy, you can't either.

The changes to come may include a tighter economy, more terrorism, more government controls upon people's travel, finances, and communications. Not directly, of course. Things are done in much more subtle ways.

Changes will be "sold" to people as a direction good for them. In fact, they're good for no one in the end. But people will buy the clever spins, because they want to see them as in their own best interests.

It's the old lie of getting something for nothing.

So in reaction to this stream of negative human consciousness in action, the forces of nature will rebel. Look for lots of changes in the next ten to fifteen years.

Why Do We Need Experiences?

If every day in my spiritual exercises I declare myself a true vehicle for God and during the course of the day I find myself in situations that don't look, seem, or feel right, what does that mean? Does it mean I need the experience for my spiritual development or that I am there to help others or that I made the wrong choice?

Every situation in your life has some spiritual purpose to it.

By doing the Spiritual Exercises of ECK every day, you open your heart and mind to the ECK, Holy Spirit, to give the experiences of most spiritual use to you.

As you've seen, not every experience is to your liking. Life is about making choices. The spiritual exercises open your awareness to see which of your decisions have a better outcome. Time and experience do teach us to make better long-term choices.

In a spiritual sense, there isn't an absolute right or wrong choice. But wait! Is that to say that anything goes? Not on your life.

The Law of Karma sees to that. Every choice, as you're learning, bears a consequence.

In a nutshell, your life today is the sum of all your past choices. So who's to blame for what? It all gets down to Number One—us—as the creator of our own fortunes and misfortunes.

Researchers have discovered two new decision centers in people other than in the head. These are the heart and intestines. That means, an individual would do well to make choices with something other than his head. He should also pay attention to "gut feelings" and to the whisperings of his heart.

Of course, these three minds receive messages from Soul. Imperfect choices mean incomplete experience. But isn't the gathering of experience the way to develop a greater degree of spiritual purity?

So, every experience is a teacher. Keep up with your spiritual exercises. They open your heart to love divine. Then all will benefit.

Every situation in your life has some spiritual purpose to it.

Chaos in the World

I am often concerned by the chaos and upheaval in the world and the apparent lack of competency in its political leaders. How can I better deal with this concern?

The point of everything is that the higher one goes spiritually, the greater becomes his vision. It then calls for an even greater state of detachment.

No matter how corrupt government becomes in any part of the world, we must do our best to rise above the moral squalor. The only way to do that is to fill yourself with love and let that love see the light of day in some way, every day.

Small kindnesses will answer, and they go a long way toward making this corrupt social creation we live in somewhat more tolerable.

Spiritual Survivor in Any Condition

You have mentioned the spiritual principle of being a survivor under any condition, if possible. How is this compatible with the spiritual principles of letting go, surrender, and just being? How do we know when to fight to survive and when to surrender and just be?

Right discrimination makes all the difference.

Right discrimination makes all the difference.

Some things naturally fall under the area of survival while others belong under surrender. For example, under which of these two headings do you suppose the five passions of the mind would fall—lust, anger, greed, attachment, and vanity? Under "surrender," not "survival," of course. And the five virtues of discrimination, forgiveness and tolerance, contentment, detachment, and humility? Under the "survival," not "surrender," area.

There is another way to state the above distinction.

Survivor applies to any God-given purpose or mission. *Surrender* means to let go of a negative or inferior state of being so that a higher one can replace it. See the difference?

People who get the survivor and surrender areas backward on purpose, especially when they apply them to the spiritual behavior of others, are plainly under the influence of the Kal, the negative force. Only they don't know that. So take any arguments by such people with a grain of salt.

Love them, but also keep away from them. They have deep spiritual problems rooted in the five passions of the mind.

National Patriotism

How do you feel about national patriotism?

This is a hard issue to address. When patriotism becomes blind emotion, it will steal people's freedom. Patriotism as a measured, rational thing is all right. It's nothing more than one's way of saying, "I like what my country is and what it stands for."

In Eckankar, we support every good government.

The United States is a product of the U.S. Constitution. It is the business plan, if you will, of the rights and responsibilities of U.S. citizens. That document was the creation of men who'd studied history and philosophy. They were not bumpkins.

Their research showed the abysmal result of earlier attempts at a republic. They had all failed.

When patriotism becomes blind emotion, it will steal people's freedom.

Ancient Greece developed the idea, but its republic collapsed when it changed, in time, to a democracy. People voted themselves more and more public pay for normal civic duties. That burgeoning democracy fell upon its own sword.

When the republic had deteriorated into a near absolute democracy, its form of government became mob rule. It had surrendered its representative form of government.

That is the danger for every republic. That was the foundation of the U.S. Nowhere does the U.S. Constitution mention a democracy. Blind patriotism often backfires. Later, to their regret, people may find they've surrendered basic rights during a hot flash of patriotic fervor. It is like a drunken stupor.

In Eckankar, we recognize the imperfection of life on earth, and we do fulfill our duties to the state. However, we're always mindful of our calling to God. It comes first.

We recognize the imperfection of life on earth, and we do fulfill our duties to the state. However, our calling to God comes first.

Becoming a Success

Recently, I started a construction business, but no matter how hard I work, most of my money seems to go for taxes. Are these taxes a violation of spiritual law? What can I do to become a success?

Let's take your concerns one by one. It doesn't take a lot of money to be a greater Co-worker with God. But you already know that. Yet it's in the cards (karma) for some individuals to have wealth and learn to deal with it, in either a spiritual or selfish way.

Taxes are taxes, neither good nor bad.

Of all the people who face the tax problem, each has a somewhat unique situation. Rich people, poor people—some pay too much, while others don't pay at all. You need either to become an expert on the changing tax laws or else find a good tax consultant (CPA or tax attorney) for expert help.

But that's beyond the scope of my advice.

Every country taxes its people to pay the cost of government. Some taxes are fair, while others burden the people, robbing them of the chance for a life of freedom and personal choice. Again, that's a social or political issue beyond the scope of my advice. People who make and enforce tax laws, and all other laws, may violate the spiritual law, but the Lords of Karma will deal with them in good time.

How can you become a success? What is success? It is happiness, and that does not depend upon wealth. There are miserable rich people as well as happy poor people, and vice versa, so don't fall for the illusion that wealth makes for bliss. Nor does it mean a greater ability to serve the Holy Spirit, the ECK.

How can you become a success? All real success is about love.

All real success is about love. Love the breath of air, for it's a gift of life. Love your work: It will expand your God-given powers of creation. And love and serve your dear ones.

A final word: Obey the two laws the writer Richard Maybury gives in *Whatever Happened to Justice?* "Do all you have agreed to do," and "Do not encroach on other persons or their property."

Success is hard to come by, but love can make it happen.

The Value of Spiritual Values

In our region the suicide rate among teenagers and young adults is one of the highest in the world. Would this be related to insufficient family and spiritual values taught to them?

The suicide rate among the youth in your region is indeed due to poor training of family and spiritual values. There are also other reasons.

Among them is the unrecognized danger of electrical currents to nerve cells by all the electronic devices that are a growing part of our cultures. These devices include cell phones and computer games. The emissions they throw off disrupt the nerve cells in the brain, especially the use of headphones for CD players and radios.

Also included as reasons for the high suicide (and growing crime) rate in some places is the normal fare of mayhem and killing seen on TV. News reports are among the worst offenders. Violence sells.

The last two words are key. Such violent stories in highly graphic detail abound because people like them.

Another cause of the high suicide rate can be a lack of sunshine, especially in countries of the north. We need a certain amount of sun every day or so. Without it, depression grows. But there are also other reasons on top of the ones above. Don't overlook the effect of high taxes. They completely destroy the incentive to work, because any effort is like paddling furiously in deep water but slowly sinking anyway. Tax slavery is a serious depressant.

All these elements destroy the survival instinct. What is the solution?

Put all these elements together, plus several others not listed here, and see the creation of negative forces that destroy the survival instinct. Hence, a high suicide rate.

What is the solution?

Precious little can change such a negative environment except the ECK teachings. So let people know of them.

Learning from the Heart

I have a teacher who does not have the best interest of her students at heart. It is difficult to learn in this type of environment. What can I do in this situation?

Some of my best teachers were monsters—or at least I thought so at the time.

Whether in school or in the workplace, we'll always run into people whose values appear to be much less than could be desired. A teacher, of course, has a duty to teach a subject. But here the human element comes in. Some teachers cannot teach, just as some students cannot learn.

Ask your classmates a question in private: Apart from this teacher, who was the worst teacher they ever had? Remember to also ask them about their best teacher.

A dull teacher can teach you patience. A hard teacher can teach the virtue of work. An unfair teacher can remind you to develop fairness with others. An incompetent teacher can teach you compassion. An insensitive teacher can teach you diplomacy and grace.

No matter what, always do your best.

A dull teacher can teach you patience. An insensitive teacher can teach you diplomacy and grace.

Celebrations in ECK

Why are there no ECK holidays, for example, Christmas, Hanukkah, or Easter? My family celebrates by getting a tree and opening presents on Christmas morning. I wish there was an ECK holiday that was special that we could celebrate with our families.

The decorated Christmas tree is a rather recent addition to the Christmas holiday. First introduced in Germany within the last few hundred years, it came a good fifteen hundred years after the birth of Christ. Long before that, the pagan Romans had a fir tree as a symbol for their messiah.

Eckankar already has a day of celebration for the ECK New Year on October 22 and for Founder's Day on September 17. More will appear in our later history.

The holiday of Christmas itself took years to establish. Its celebration was first in January and was more widespread by AD 100. Later, the church fathers settled on December 25 as the date to celebrate Christ's birth.

Japan boasts over two hundred holidays, both religious and civil, every year. It has a long history as a country.

A culture or a society takes many years to develop its celebrations. Be open to holidays and festivals that are a part of your society. I like to celebrate Thanksgiving. Someday ECKists will include it as one of their holidays too. And why not enjoy a Christmas dinner with your family?

Life is a movable feast. It depends neither upon a set day nor season, but upon your love for living.

The point is that a true holiday is a celebration of God's love for Soul. A holiday, then, is any gathering, even a birthday party, that is our thank-you to God and the ECK (Holy Spirit) for the gift of life.

Make sure the holiday celebration is planned as a happy event. That day, be on your best behavior. It's an ideal day to practice joy, good humor, laughter, and song.

Life is a movable feast. It depends neither upon a set day nor season, but upon your love for living. That love should reflect your humble love for God.

Staying Infused with Light and Sound

You wrote about the world collective consciousness choosing warfare and social welfare and its effects. Has this planet refused the Causal initiation? And how may we best live here?

The world consciousness is in a terrible struggle to reach the Causal Plane. Like an individual's initiation rigors, those of the world community are equally exacting.

Causal Plane. It means the place of prime causes. At question there is the issue of taking responsibility for one's own deeds. Instead a trend is for world leaders to make apologies for things their country did before they were born or when they were still children. On the other hand, they quickly break the law to escape responsibility for their own misdeeds.

All that's fine. What any world leader does, however, depends upon the support of a majority of his people. (The majority may either be one of force or numbers.) When a nation supports a leader who refuses to accept responsibility for his misdeeds, his people share in that spiritual failure.

Even worse, a negative wave, by its popular support, shows that its influence is pervasive among a people. It is a destructive force. None who support such a state will advance spiritually.

Rather, they soon fall back.

Whenever there is widespread support for a strong and effective channel of the Kal, the negative force, in some key role of leadership, it speaks reams about his supporters. How can it be that people infused with the Sound and Light of God would support a strong Kal agent, and do it with a passion?

The simple answer is that they're no longer

At question is the issue of taking responsibility for one's own deeds.

infused with the Sound and Light of God. They've fallen right into the Kal trap of illusion.

This would seem to paint a bleak picture. It would be a bleak picture, indeed, except that the ECK teachings are for the individual. The group is incidental: It is only a reflection of the collective state of the individuals within it.

Yes, stars still shine in the night. So do the Spiritual Exercises of ECK. They lift you into the Sound and Light of God.

The Wind of Change

Recently we experienced weeks of extreme weather: hurricanes, one right after the other. People felt their lives were turned upside down. Many of us have speculated on the waking dream behind this, and we feel it was the Wind of Change blowing away the deadwood (attitudes and attachments) and the unnecessary (plans, projects, ideas that are not essential). We see the tremendous amount of rain as Divine Spirit coming in to wash away the debris and cleanse the land—our communities and consciousness.

But we know we only see the tip of the iceberg. Could you share a deeper understanding?

It is heartening to see how you and a growing number of others can trace the movement of the ECK (Holy Spirit) as It sweeps across the land.

This planet and its people are certainly seeing and feeling the turbulent winds of spiritual purification.

This planet and its people are certainly seeing and feeling the turbulent winds of spiritual purification.

So what's going on?

There's more on the line than the simple issue

of whether earth's climate is seeing a global warm-ing or cooling. The fact is that extremes of heating and cooling are both occurring, often in the very same year.

So what is going on?

Earth is trembling from the extremes of heat and cold, wind and wave, volcano and earthquake. The forces of nature are quick-stepping at an ever-faster rate. They leave people trembling, in terror for their lives.

Some speculation has it that earth's magnetic poles are switching. If that proves to be the case, then the next ten years and beyond will see a lot more disruptions and upheavals.

These are days for all to sharpen their spiritual vision and hearing.

These are days for all to sharpen their spiritual vision and hearing.

Service in the Military

I am considering joining the military as a pilot to earn my way in this world. But how can joining this kind of entity—one that, in essence, trains one to take the lives of others, subjugate and encroach on people and their property—lead to spiritual unfoldment? I understand the human right to de-fend what is held dear, but where lies the fine line between defense and encroachment? Or, more impor-tantly, the line between spiritual advancement and spiritual deterioration? What real reason can one with a heart of gold have to pull a trigger in any scenario? It leaves me very conflicted.

Other young people thinking about signing up for military service may harbor the same reserva-tions as you, especially pilots.

Pilot training is very costly. A branch of military service can help pay the tab. But joining up involves conditions, which may well mean taking people's lives. So choose carefully.

Interview school counselors to learn what options are open to you. Do they include openings for candidates who rescue, rather than destroy, others? Also speak with military recruiters. What guarantees do they offer that you will actually end up with the sort of duty that you want? This applies to all branches of service.

Let's say, by some chance, you end up in an area that is not of your choosing. Take it as a golden opportunity to learn spiritual detachment. Look always to the ECK.

No experience is ever lost, so seek out the good in all things and all people.

No experience is ever lost, so seek out the good in all things and all people.

The Spiritual Significance of Cloning

What is the spiritual significance (if any) of cloning?

Cloning raises huge public outcries today. Yet someday it's likely to raise no more eyebrows that news of a transplanted tooth, heart, or eye.

Blood transfusions once faced a challenge by religious minds. Blood—the life blood—was an integral part of one's essence, and to mix it with that of another person was to play God. And there were setbacks in the early days. Patients with transfusions died. Religionists knew it for a visitation of God. But then, scientists unraveled the mystery of blood types. Compatible types saved lives.

So it will be with cloning.

Cloning is moving along two roads. First is the

duplication of a whole animal. The second, a development of the first, aims at reproducing body parts. The idea here is to create a body laboratory and warehouse, a place where doctors have immediate access to hearts, livers, lungs, etc. No patient, it is hoped, need die while waiting months for a suitable donor. All the same, many ethical questions do lie in the fore.

There will be failures at first with cloning. Some clones today experience unnaturally short lives or rapid aging. Scientists will overcome most problems, as in the case of transfusions. But new ones will crop up. This is earth.

One expectation of science about reproducing a perfect double will, I suspect, meet with perplexity and dismay. Though a clone's skin will be identical to the original's, the indefinable personality and behavior will be as puzzling as is the fact of a good son and a wayward son with the same advantages of family and upbringing.

Science thus creeps a bit closer to the unique nature of Soul, an independent being at the heart of all creation.

Lessons from the Past

In a talk you referred to Saint Paul and the complex task he faced as the architect of Christianity. There are many parallels to establishing a religion of the Light and Sound of God. How do you see the future potential for Eckankar as a world religion?

The laying of a foundation for every religion has a similar history. A messenger brings a message from on high. At first, only a few in society recognize

Science creeps a bit closer to the unique nature of Soul, an independent being at the heart of all creation.

the far-reaching importance of the message, and of them, maybe only one or two get it mostly right.

In the beginning this kernel of truth reaches only a handful of disciples. But in time the master gives them small tasks to test their abilities and provide an opportunity for growth. The message soon bumps the sides of the envelope. It must get out. So the master sends the ablest disciples to venture among the people with the new truths. Likely as not, they return a bit battered. They report the mixed results to the master, who tells of means to avoid or meet such challenges on the next trip out.

The early disciples thus become carriers of the word. It falls to them to teach new willing hands to help in the master's mission.

Disputes then arise. One group of believers charges another group with distorting the original message of the master, who is long gone.

Then a champion arises among them. He looks at the charges and countercharges, studies the history of this religion, couples that with knowledge gleaned from the missteps of earlier religions at that level of development, and issues a ruling agreeable to most. This process of the assimilation of knowledge and experience, and their consolidation (so they can sink into the group's consciousness), goes on in perpetuity.

There is a big difference between ECK and other paths. A Living ECK Master is the experienced traveler.

Yet there is a big difference between ECK and other paths. A Living ECK Master is the experienced traveler. He, like past ECK Masters, is the eternal, Living Word Itself. Thus truth is not left in the care of leaders with an imperfect understanding.

If the foundation is strong, Eckankar is destined to become a world religion.

Love Crowds Out Evil

*The Eckankar dictionary (*A Cosmic Sea of Words: The ECKANKAR Lexicon*) says Kali is the "mother of Kal" and also that "in Christianity she is the virgin mother, the mother of saviors of the world but not the ECK Masters, who are born of ECK power."*

I have many Catholic cousins, and they regard the Blessed Mother as a supremely spiritual being. Who is this Kali, and how can she be perceived in such different ways?

Please understand that neither the Kal (negative power) nor the Kali are evil in the way usually thought of.

Yes, the Kal is Satan, the devil.

Why would a loving, all-powerful God let a destructive twerp like that run around loose without a bridle on? Because he and his deeds test the spiritual strength of people. In fact, his mischief helps them grow. Satan is part of God's plan and not a diabolical error.

So the devil gets a bad rap.

Satan is, rather, the king of illusions. He gets people to believe in falsehoods ("you can get something for nothing"). Until they learn to see through the smoke and mirrors he sets up to fool them, they'll happily cheat, lie, steal, and do other wrong things.

Someday, though, these deeds must be paid up in full. It's the day of reckoning. A moment of "Aha, now I see!" An enlightenment. A graduation to a new level.

Another test passed on Soul's journey home to God.

The Kal (negative power) and his deeds test the spiritual strength of people. Satan is the king of illusions.

Respect your cousins' belief. You and your cousins are on different legs of the same journey home to God.

Respect your cousins' belief in the Blessed Mother Mary. Hers is a kindly face that gives hope and love in a harsh world that could otherwise turn good people toward bitterness. Their love is the important thing here.

You see, love crowds out evil. When their hearts are full of love for the Blessed Mother, they are better for it spiritually.

You and your cousins are on different legs of the same journey home to God.

Setting a Good Example

I am an ECKist who lives close to the Temple of ECK in Chanhassen, Minnesota. I get a lot of criticism at school about my religion. People say I worship the devil, that ECKists are Antichrists, that I am evil, and negative things about the Temple of ECK.

Can you give me some insights on how to respond to these criticisms?

Hatred is a terrible thing. We know that the criticisms are false. Some people and their kids are not living up to the teachings of Christ.

Christ taught love, not hatred.

"Thou shalt love thy neighbour as thyself," he said. (So do they not love themselves that they hate you?) Christ called this quote the second commandment (Matt. 22:39).

Christ also said, "He that is without sin among you, let him first cast a stone at her" (John 8:7).

Again, he said, "Love your enemies," in Matt. 5:44.

Understand, the Law of Love applies to all. That

includes ECKists. So your classmates break this Law of Love by their hatred of you. God will deal with them through the Lords of Karma, who impartially judge each action.

Don't be a sheep at school. You must be the model of love that Christ taught, even as all true masters teach their disciples to be carriers of love.

You must set a good example.

If you tell a classmate (who says false things about you) one of Christ's sayings above, he will catch himself. But only if that classmate is close to Christ's teachings. It could be that some only practice their religion in church on Sunday, but in their hearts are all the things they accuse you of.

It's tough. Perhaps you'll gain strength from your experiences, for we make our own heavens.

But don't be a rug for others' muddy feet either. If things get too rough at school, keep your parents up to speed. They may be able to help through other means.

Above all, chant HU, the sacred name of God, silently when trouble comes at school. I am with you, you know.

Fulfilling Our Goals

How can we fulfill our spiritual mission, or live our dreams, if they seem unreachable?

Let us just say that good things do not always come easy. At times, it may seem as if our goals are diametrically opposed to one another, to make us break out our creative imagination and put it to good use.

And, often as not, that is the case.

Our goals make us break out our creative imagination and put it to good use.

A "can-do" attitude goes a long way toward fulfilling any dream or purpose. At the heart of it, you are trying to attain some truth. The idea is that if you fulfill a certain goal, you'll be better off for it spiritually. And you would be too.

But, say your dream or goal needs fine-tuning for it to be of the utmost good. The ECK will do that for you.

Yet the human consciousness may see the necessary inner changes as failure, a disheartening prospect to say the least. However, in this lies a test. Will you stand or will you fall?

How great is your resolve?

How strong is your faith in the ECK?

How much do you love life?

No matter what, set out boldly on your journey. Count every obstacle a blessing. And above all things, love the holy Presence that is always with you.

> *A "can-do" attitude goes a long way toward fulfilling any dream or purpose.*

You are Soul. Know that you are a spark of God and can exist fully only within the realization of that profound truth.

2
WHO ARE
YOU AS SOUL?

What is Soul, and why are we here?

Soul just is. It is the creative center of Its own world.

We know that Soul exists by the evidence of life around us. When Soul inhabits a body, that body lives, moves, and has being. When Soul leaves, the body no longer lives, moves, or has being. What has left? By direct or indirect evidence, we know that some unseen force gives life to a physical body.

What is that something? Soul, of course.

Opinions about Soul outnumber people's opinions about politics. People who *know*—actually know, not just believe—that Soul outlives death enjoy happy, creative lives. The rest are miserable and afraid.

People who fear hell fall for the trap that Soul can be burned by fire. That's really sad. Soul exists because God loves It. Its destiny is to become a Co-worker with God.

Soul is the creative center of Its own world. Its destiny is to become a Co-worker with God.

Plato told of the separation of Soul from the body. The old Greek mystery schools taught their students that Soul could reach the altar of God through certain secret methods. The students spent a few minutes a day with unique contemplative exercises that opened them little by little to the Light and Sound of God. That gave them unshakable proof that Soul lives forever.

The most important point of all is that you are Soul. Know that you are a spark of God and can exist fully only within the realization of that profound truth. As such, you are a light and inspiration to others.

When Was Soul Created?

Did God create all Souls at the same time? If yes, why? And if not, why not?

God, also known as Sugmad in the ancient teachings, created Souls before time began.

In our world, we must think about time. Even your question says "at the same time." But God, also known as Sugmad in the ancient teachings, created Souls before time began, so it is not a question of Souls made sooner or later. As humans, we find this hard to understand.

Yet even when studying the origin of this universe, scientists run into a problem of how to determine the age of the big bang. It's a theory about the moment of creation. But creation happened before there was time. So scientists work from there and accept the fact of creation, because the evidence is all around. However, they cannot fix a date to the beginning of time. It's simply not possible.

Sugmad created all Souls before time began, so there is no answer to your question of when. If God creates more Souls, that also happens beyond the laws of time and space.

There is no simple reply to your question. But spiritually, there is an answer. In contemplation, ask the Mahanta, the Inner Master, to let you see and know about the creation and nature of Soul. If you are sincere, he will show you.

What Is Our Nature as Soul?

I have many questions about the nature of Soul. For example, do minerals, plants, and animals have Souls?

An uncountable number of Souls exist in creation. There is also an endless number of forms in which Souls can find expression for spiritual unfoldment. The human form is but one of many.

On earth, we are familiar mainly with human, animal, reptile, fish, plant, and even mineral forms (like rocks, etc.).

We are a little like the theologians and others of the early Middle Ages. They believed that all human races were then known. Of course, the sea explorations by Columbus and others later revealed two whole continents (North and South America) inhabited by a previously unknown red race. That discovery was a major threat to biblical interpretation. Red people? The Bible didn't say anything about a red race.

The Christian Bible says nothing about Souls inhabiting forms other than humans either. Nor does it say anything about Souls living on other planets in forms not quite human. Yet Souls do.

Soul can take many different approaches to reach purification. A Soul that today inhabits an animal form will later be offered other life-forms, perhaps even human, when It is ready for a higher stage.

There is an endless number of forms in which Souls can find expression for spiritual unfoldment. The human form is but one of many.

Entering a human body on the physical plane is indeed an optimal experience for all Souls who are given that choice. But the same is also true for Souls who are given the choice to enter an animal or plant form.

The point: Everything is within its rightful place in the Kingdoms of God.

Since Soul is invisible, for the most part, and not subject to analysis in a scientific laboratory, Its nature remains a matter of speculative belief or personal experience.

The purpose of the Eckankar teachings is to give the individual proof of the nature of Soul in a way that is meaningful to him. When and how this is done depends upon the Mahanta, who determines the best time and place.

Does Soul Live Forever?

How do you know Soul really lives forever and doesn't just die, or stop? How do you know you'll go to another world or another life?

A mature Soul knows Its eternal nature.

Your question has been a sore spot for atheists (don't believe in God) and agnostics (don't know whether God exists) for a long time.

In a nutshell, a mature Soul knows Its eternal nature. An immature Soul does not. Those who have the spiritual maturity to be convinced will be convinced in good time, but the others will take a few lifetimes longer.

There is a book you'll find helpful in meeting your own doubts. Some of the writer's philosophy may be tough wading for you, but the case histories he gives of people's experiences *between* lives are very interesting. I think you'll like it.

The name of the book is *Journey of Souls* by Dr. Michael Newton (Llewellyn Publications, St. Paul, Minnesota).

Who Was Here First?

Who was the first person? How did that person get here?

The first person had no name. Speech, of course, had not developed yet, because names are like labels that people create to call one and not another. So, speech takes people, more than one. Even more than two or three or four, or so.

It took a long time before people dreamed up names.

How did the first person get here?

To get the answer, we ask, "So how did the first *two* people, or more, come into bodies in the high Mental Plane?" (Everything here comes in twos.) They materialized. It was a bit like on the TV show *Star Trek*, where explorers in spaceships beam down to a planet.

They just seem to appear as if by magic. Yet there are laws of science at work that allow for an orderly transfer of the atoms that make up a human body.

That's to say, people today have a lot to learn about the laws of science. But the knowledge is growing by tiny steps.

The first people on each plane were created by the Holy Spirit, the ECK, through the arts and sciences of spiritual workers on the plane above. So people on the Astral Plane had the responsibility of seeing to the ways and means of transferring Astral Plane people to the Physical Plane.

To get the answer, we ask, "How did the first two people, *or more, come into bodies?"*

What means did they use?

Here, I must direct you to *The Shariyat-Ki-Sugmad*, Book One. First, read the first two pages of chapter 1, "The ECK—The Divine Voice of Sugmad." That's to get a sense of how creation began.

The background for mankind's development on earth is a fascinating study.

Second, read chapter 3, "The Doctrine of the ECK Marg." This chapter of the Way of the Eternal, the holy scriptures of ECK, gives the background for mankind's development on earth. It does *not* say the actual way the first couples got here. You can make that connection yourself. People's consciousness, helped by TV and movie space-travel shows, is now ready to see *one* way that the first people came to earth.

It is a fascinating study. At night, please be sure to watch your dreams. Often they fill in some of the details not recorded in *The Shariyat*.

How Life Began

Can you please tell me how life on earth began? If it came from another planet, how did it begin there? If God created life, how did It do it?

Believe it or not, people of all faiths have asked this question in one form or another ever since the dawn of history. All religions have their own answers.

Our scientists run all over the globe in a search for the oldest human fossils. They want to know the age of humans. Once they learn that, they hope to tackle the big question: How did the first human come to be?

The answer would shake the main religions to the core.

Way back, there was no earth, no creation. But Sugmad (God) wanted a place to educate Souls, so the ECK (the Word of God) began to create things. It did so by changing the vibrations of Light and Sound in a certain region. That area became the lower worlds.

First was the Light and Sound of God. Then, at a lower step of vibration, came the gases. Eons of time later, liquids and solid matter began to form: the building blocks of lower creation. The Etheric Plane was the first plane to appear, then the Mental Plane. Much later came this Physical Plane.

Galaxies and planets were the first to form on each plane, and then the ECK began to experiment with life-forms. On earth, these included the dinosaurs.

In the meantime, the ECK had evolved higher life-forms, like humans, on the Etheric Plane. They began to seed the planets there by establishing colonies of mind travelers, who could move from place to place without slow, clumsy spacecraft.

Those people pushed back the frontiers of space, even as our astronauts do today. With colonies all throughout the Etheric Plane, the early ECK Masters began to open a new frontier: travel between the Etheric and Mental dimensions. So the seeding of colonies now began on the Mental Plane.

Visitors from space seeded Earth with the first colonies. There was no first man or woman. A spaceship brought a small group of people here to start a colony. Then somewhere down the line came you.

Someday, and not too far off, knowledge of this seeding of the planets will be common knowledge among people of higher spiritual awareness.

Someday this seeding of the planets will be common knowledge.

Expanding Awareness

Why did Soul have to come into the lower worlds? Did it do something bad in heaven and have to be punished?

Thank you for your thoughtful question about Soul and Its arrival in the lower worlds. These Souls did nothing so *bad* as to have to be sent here, except that they needed to move to the next phase in God's purpose for creating them. Please understand that the true spiritual worlds above the Fifth (Soul) Plane do not come under the laws of logic from the Mental Plane. You may or may not have trouble understanding this.

Sugmad (God) created Souls so that It could come into an expanding awareness of Itself through their experiences of *love and mercy* toward others. See?

The Souls at play in the spiritual worlds fulfilled a part of God's self-discovery (if we can even use that word). After watching Souls at play for a while (again, time and space have no relevance in the spiritual worlds. They are merely a convenience for us when trying to communicate in human languages—all still from the Mental Plane), Sugmad was ready for a whole new level of an expanding awareness of Itself. Soul exists because God loves It.

This element of God—expanding awareness—also underlies the "plus element" of the ECK teachings. That is, there is always one more heaven. Always one more state of consciousness above the last.

Being Conscious

The simplest key to being "conscious" is the art of listening.

A goal of mine as Soul is to become a conscious Co-worker with God. I try to put love into all my thoughts and actions, yet "being conscious" seems to elude me. How can I attain full consciousness, both in the inner and outer worlds?

The simplest key to being "conscious" is the art of listening. By all means listen to others, but also listen—and watch—for the silent voice of the Mahanta, the Inner Master, that speaks through others, the waking dream, and intuition, for example.

To be conscious is to be humble and compassionate in the presence of life. In short, love fills your being. The ego is out.

Working with Polarity

As a sports fan (tennis in particular), when watching two opponents compete, I often find myself siding with one particular person. Somehow, this makes the match more thrilling and worthwhile seeing. When the match or game is over, however, whether my favorite player won or not, I accept the result, with no hard feelings.

Do my feelings or opinions when watching a match or game conflict with what is meant to happen? Is it really important for all concerned to keep myself completely neutral when viewing sports?

Polarity is one of the features of life in the worlds below the Soul Plane. Of course you can pick sides in a tennis match, soccer game, or in the political arena.

As an aware spiritual being, however, you should be able to stop taking sides when your participation could take a negative turn. Let's say, for example, you root for a soccer team. But the crowd's emotions heat up, and the result is a riot. Don't join in.

You do have a balanced spiritual outlook when you can accept a loss by a favorite player without hard feelings. You're on the right track.

Your feelings or opinions have no more or less of an impact upon the outcome of a match or game than do those of someone else. So don't worry about it. Sit back and enjoy the game.

To be conscious is to be humble and compassionate in the presence of life. Love fills your being.

Becoming Aware of Ourselves

Do we experience the higher worlds by having our awareness encompass the entire plane? If there is no separation between ourselves as Soul and the higher plane we are in, when we go to a Temple of Golden Wisdom, are we actually becoming aware of a part of ourselves on that plane?

Soul's awareness can ultimately only expand.

Soul's state of consciousness is a reflection of Its awareness. In the pure spiritual worlds, where it is impossible to speak in dualistic or negative terms, we can only say that Soul's awareness is the sum of Its awareness of Its relationship with Sugmad (God). That awareness can ultimately only expand.

Soul's perception of a plane in the higher worlds is one of quality rather than quantity. In other words, Soul comes to a gradual appreciation of the subtleties found there instead of digesting pieces of them, like a meal. It is hard to put into words.

Progression implies some sort of change despite the fact that we're speaking of the higher worlds. Without progression there couldn't be lesser or more unfolded spiritual beings—yet there are. Also, if there were no limits in the higher worlds (not a higher-world concept, by the way), there would not be a succession of planes there. Yet, in a sense, there are.

The difficulty, of course, in speaking about conditions in the higher worlds is that the Law of Love which operates there is beyond human language or logic. So the Spiritual Exercises of ECK, an adventurous spirit, and complete faith in the Mahanta, the Inner Master, become your key to understanding the unique conditions of the higher worlds, including those that surround a Temple of Golden Wisdom there.

What about Soul Mates?

I read in the book The Tiger's Fang, *by Paul Twitchell, about the topic of Soul mates, and it baffles me. Does that mean that every Soul will somehow find his Soul mate somewhere on the journey to Sugmad?*

Your question does come up fairly often, so let's take a look at it.

The confusion arises from something Paul Twitchell once wrote in chapter 6 of *The Tiger's Fang*. There, he endorsed the idea. But Paul was then still a Master in training. His understanding was incomplete.

Later he strongly reversed himself in *The ECK-Vidya, Ancient Science of Prophecy*. You'll surely want to read chapter 5, "The ECK-Vidya Theory of Time Twins." He wrote it as a spiritually mature individual. Over the years, too, I have addressed this issue in a number of talks and writings.

The time-twin, or Soul-mate, theory is an occult invention. As such, it has no grounding in the ECK teachings. The masculine and feminine principles are within each one of us. But such a division, or separation, is a phenomenon of the lower worlds and does not exist in the higher ones.

Let's look at the origin of the Soul-mate theory.

The Soul-mate theory arose because some people in early history were quite aware of an emptiness inside themselves. An individual with strong masculine forces driving him might feel an insensitivity to things. So he searched for a Soul mate with whom he'd feel like a whole being.

All that changes during Self-Realization. When an individual reaches the Soul Plane, the masculine

When an individual reaches the Soul Plane, the masculine and feminine principles unite within him. Then he is made whole.

and feminine principles unite within him. Then he is made whole.

Once you know the truth about this Soul-mate theory, you can save yourself a lot of heartache in selecting a mate.

Birth and Death

Since birth and death mark an entrance into the physical and exit from it, is it the same at translation (death) for the next world? In other words, are we born as infants in the next world when we translate (die) from this one? It seems from reading and experience that you are in the next world as you were at translation from this one, e.g., adult here, then adult there. Could you give me some clarity on this?

Yes and no and maybe.

A more complete answer is in *The Slow Burning Love of God*, Mahanta Transcripts, Book 13, where I describe Linda's trip to the Causal Plane and "The Slide of Reincarnation."

I'd like to give a direct answer to your question, but you'll get a far better understanding in this excerpt from chapter 6 of that book:

These Souls get on this slide of reincarnation and go sliding right back into another body on earth.

She saw these long chutes or slides, like farmers use in barn lofts for dropping hay to the cattle below. Souls, looking like adult human beings, were standing at the top of the slide. As they slid down, they kept changing form until they became infants. Then they'd plop down into the world, crying and wondering what had happened. It was a cold, dark world after the light of the Causal Plane.

These Souls had been adults who had died on earth and gone to the Causal Plane to await their time of reincarnation. They'd get on this slide of reincarnation and go sliding right back into another body on earth. But the babies only had a small memory in the back of their minds of who and what they'd been in their previous lives.

Linda realized that the death of the physical body here on earth is not the death of the personality. The personality lives beyond the death of the human body.

We're not talking about Soul now, we're talking about the personality: the Astral, Causal, and Mental bodies of the individual. Not until Soul is reincarnated does the personality die. This is why so many times after a parent or a loved one dies, people have dream experiences with them.

Why? They are seeing these people as the personality, or the complex that the personality stands for, meaning the Astral or Causal body.

At the base level, the physical body dies. People then take up residence on the Astral Plane. It's pretty much the same as here on earth, except they may take on a younger appearance. But the personality itself is extinguished when they go down the slide of reincarnation and come back to earth.

This explains why you see your loved ones or even pets in your dreams after they have passed on.

Not until Soul is reincarnated does the personality die. This is why you see your loved ones or even pets in your dreams after they pass on.

Who Greets a Departing Soul?

In the ECK writings, reference is made to the Angel of Death. Some of these references portray this figure in unsettling terms. Elsewhere, the writings indicate the noninitiated are met by friends and loved ones at the time of passing and guided across by a benign angelic being. Could you say a little about the experience of death for the noninitiated and what this special time means for the ECK initiate?

Good question! A rule about what happens to a noninitiate at the time of death is that there are *no* fixed rules.

Many times, the departed is greeted by loved ones. The love bond between them provides both courage and comfort.

Many times, the departed is greeted by loved ones. They come because of the love bond that exists between them. This bond, of course, is due to strong, good relationships that may date back over many centuries. Yet it provides both courage and comfort. The courage is necessary at the moment of translation, for Soul is leaving behind all things It had, in that lifetime, come to regard as essential to Its physical existence.

And, in a real sense, that is true. All those "things" were like cables, holding Soul to earth like a ship's anchors. Death cuts those cables. Without the presence of loved ones, this could prove to be an unsettling passage for some noninitiates.

Another who might greet a departing Soul is a holy man. The two have enjoyed a close relationship, making possible their monumental reunion on the other side. Satan, or one of his agents, is the player at the death of one who has committed a serious crime, like a murder. Needless to say, this spells a rueful and terrifying encounter for the departing Soul.

Happy, however, is the ECKist. He is overjoyed at the appearance of the Mahanta, who may bring others that share a spiritual bond with the ECKist.

Soul's Sound

Does Soul have a sound?

When we're on the inner planes and we hear the ECK (the Voice of God), is that us, Soul, or is it the Mahanta? How can we tell the difference? Or when we hear the Sound, is it our own sound and the Mahanta simultaneously, like being part of the body of the Mahanta?

You're making it all too complicated.

The Sound Current encompasses all sounds. The Mahanta is the ECK, thus he is also the sum of all celestial sounds.

Soul comes into harmony, or agreement, with a single sound, maybe two or three, when It reaches certain levels of unfoldment. These levels, in turn, directly relate to a given plane, or heaven. That's the place or state of consciousness at which Soul takes Its spiritual nourishment.

Even as Soul is of the body of the Holy Spirit (ECK), so is It also of the body of the Mahanta, the divine agent of God's love made manifest.

Yet Soul is not the whole body any more than a man's toe is the sum of the man. See?

Soul comes into harmony with a single sound when It reaches certain levels of unfoldment.

Animals and Heaven

When animals meet their goal, do they become ECK Masters the way we do? Where is heaven? What is heaven?

Souls in animal forms do not get the initiations as we do. Their spiritual unfoldment is handled in other ways.

Animals can follow their own path to mastership if they want to. Only through the lower worlds, though. For example, earth allows several levels for Soul to gain experiences in life, including the mineral, plant, fish, animal, and human stages.

But there's no fixed spiritual law about a rock having to stay a rock. Or a daisy staying a daisy.

By choice, though, most Souls want to taste life at all levels. They do go from the lower to higher body forms. So animals could move up to human. Yet that would take many lifetimes.

Sometimes, in a spirit of fun, we ask, "Why on earth would a cat want to be a kid? It's more fun to be a cat."

(But do you think a cat would go back to being a mouse? Probably not.)

Heaven is inside us. No one can point to a place and say, "It's here," or "It's there." It is a state of consciousness. As Soul moves to higher states of consciousness, It may choose to live and serve in places of more love and beauty. So people think that heaven is a place.

Heaven is not a place. It is a state of consciousness.

Higher Souls may live in finer places.

Yet heaven is not a place. It is a state of consciousness.

To give you an example, a child born into a family of wealth may enjoy every pleasure and still be unhappy. A sort of hell.

Again, a poor country child may be very happy with so many things to see and do. A heaven on earth.

There are few fixed rules about Soul's path to God, as humans understand them. Yet they exist.

Heart and Mind

Our minds play such an important role in our lives, and they have a place. But in serious situations how do you know when to listen to your heart instead of just the facts and information inside your head? How do you know when your heart is speaking (and not just fear or sympathy)?

You've hit upon the whole problem of living. When does one listen to the heart or the head?

If it's any consolation to you, that's the great mystery which ages upon ages of people have struggled to understand. In a pure sense the two camps, which include everyone, are the head and the heart people. But no one's all one or the other.

From what I've seen, those who are mostly head, or mind, people have a harder time in trying to deal with the hard questions of life.

Some of these hard questions include: What is love? Does God really exist? Is there life after death? In each case a mind person wants proof. Until it comes he takes the position: Since I don't know the answer, no one else can either.

Even more, a mind person is likely to go out of his way to destroy the beliefs of others. So a mind person is apt to be rigid and unforgiving in regard to the beliefs of others. A mind person is basically of a juvenile mind. He's still young in spiritual experience.

The heart person takes what life has to offer and is grateful for its blessings. Life is relatively simple for him. (Oddly, a mind person probably considers a heart person a simpleminded fool.)

But no matter. A heart person tends toward love, patience, and tolerance. He is like sunshine to others.

Head person: When faced with a complicated knot in a rope, he tries to unravel each strand.

Heart person: Like Alexander the Great, he simply cuts the rope and conquers all. Because he's rich in spiritual experience, he quickly gets to the heart of things.

The heart person takes what life has to offer and is grateful for its blessings.

Your Goals as Soul

For me, Self-Realization is mostly a concept and not a strong goal at this time. Is it OK to use ECK to improve my life without focusing on Self- and God-Realization? Also, I'm not sure what it means to really love God. How can I develop a loving relationship with God?

Put your attention upon divine love. Put your love into the things you do. Give your love to your dear ones.

In time, divine love will take you to the top of the spiritual mountain.

Love is all there is. It is the beginning and end of life. Ask the Mahanta, the Inner Master, to guide you in the ways of God's love, and life will bring you every experience needed. That is the easy way.

In time, divine love will take you to the top of the spiritual mountain. There, you will experience the wonders of Self- and God-Realization in the proper seasons of your life. And, in the end, you will love God completely.

Accept each dream as a spiritual gift. Roll it gently around in your mind to see if loving patience on your part will reveal its significance.

3
UNDERSTANDING YOUR DREAMS

How do the dream teachings of Eckankar differ from other dream teachings?

Dream teachings range from the silly to the highly mental. All can help people to some degree, depending upon where that person is. The dream teachings of ECK follow the basic pattern of all the ECK teachings—they are grounded both in the physical teaching as well as the spiritual, inner, subtle side.

Finding the Dream Lesson

Sometimes I have trouble finding the lesson or message in my dreams. Some of them seem just too wacky to even have one! Does each dream have a spiritual meaning or lesson involved? Or are some just purely creations of my imagination?

Every experience, waking or dream, has a lesson or message to impart to us. But let the meanings of your inner and outer experiences come naturally.

Every experience, waking or dream, has a lesson or message to impart to us.

47

In other words, if the lesson or message isn't clear, don't force it.

Soul, the spiritual self that you are, will send another dream again in some other way until your human self can easily grasp the meaning.

In Eckankar, dream study works on all levels. As with all things of a divine nature, accept each dream as a spiritual gift. Wonder about it. Roll it gently around in your mind to see if loving patience on your part will reveal its significance.

Dream experiences are real experiences from another time, place, or dimension.

This approach is the reason the Eckankar spiritual studies are called the Easy Way.

One other point.

Dream experiences are real experiences from another time, place, or dimension. Some of them are from past lives, which you'd expect to be straightforward. Yet here's where the mind—or what you called "just purely creations of my imagination?"—comes in.

The dream censor is a function, or part, of the mind. For purely karmic reasons, it may decide that a certain past life would be too much of a shock to you. You might break off a relationship. Yet that relationship in the present time may be necessary to bring an important insight to you.

So the dream censor tones down dreams. It lets a dreamer go ahead with life and so profit from past-life experiences.

Are Dreams Real?

I've noticed that when you write about your own dream experiences, you often speak of them as real experiences on the inner planes, which you've referred to as "Soul journeys" rather than dreams. When you

*share the dream experiences of ECK initiates, it seems
you often speak of those dreams in symbolic terms.*

*As a person unfolds spiritually, do their dreams
become less symbolic? Also, what is the source of a
chela's dream content? Are all dreams constructed
or influenced by the Dream Master, or is the content
sometimes determined simply by where we put our
attention on the inner planes?*

A Soul journey is a real experience. A dream is
a mere shade of it, to a degree, for the protection of
the dreamer upon awakening. The dream censor
tries to avoid shocks.

Moving on, a waking dream is a spiritual insight
that's contained in a memorable experience.

So we place an inner and outer experience side
by side and realize that each may reveal divine
knowledge about, or insight into, a troubling condition or situation. Yet each is also a stand-alone
experience. An inner waking dream, at its level, is
every bit as valid as an outer one.

Now let's make a jump.

Some people think that "illusion" means "not
real." Stub your toe or hit a finger with a hammer,
and you'll think otherwise.

The true meaning of "illusion" is "not seen correctly or seen in a false light."

Here, a bigger jump.

Any experience, inner or outer, may carry with
it a divine message: an aid to spiritual unfoldment.
This is one of many benefits that come to a chela
(student) of ECK. A waking dream is a gift.

The source of a chela's dream content? Another
jump.

It's from one of his material sheaths, bodies, on

*Some think
"illusion"
means "not
real." The
true meaning
is "not seen
correctly or
seen in a
false light."*

a higher spirito-material plane. The Mahanta, the Inner Master, takes a snapshot of a *dynamic* experience there and delivers it to the dreamer, who often awakens to ask, *What was that? Where'd it come from?*

Your question is a big foot for the small shoe of this question-and-answer format. Want more? Please ask.

Water Dreams

Water in dreams often means spiritual purification.

I keep having recurring dreams with water. What does this symbolize?

Water in dreams often means spiritual purification.

It may foretell an outer ECK initiation, or a minor inner initiation before the next outer one.

When a dream of water comes to you, it is a reminder to again dedicate yourself to the ECK, Divine Spirit. This is a very good dream to have, especially when the body of water is like an ocean. It suggests the Ocean of Love and Mercy.

Are the People in Dreams Real?

People in my dreams never act the way they do in real life. Why? Am I really with that person on the inner, or not? When I dream of other people, is it about them or what they represent to me? How can I distinguish between the two? How do I find a balance between the dream world and my physical life? If I have a disturbing dream about someone, how can I understand the spiritual gift and then let it go?

You really are with that person on the inner. But a couple of things come into play.

First, you may not remember the inner experience exactly as it happened. The dream censor is responsible for that. He represents the social part of the Kal, the negative force. His reason is that you're not ready to handle the truth—which may be true. So your recall is clouded. That's illusion. It protects you from emotional shocks.

Second, your distorted recall of the dream will *represent* a hidden truth, instead of giving the actual truth face-to-face. So you must decipher it by asking the Mahanta, the Inner Master, for help in understanding. Ask him for help during contemplation.

Every well-balanced person finds a balance between the dream world and the physical life. Remember, the physical laws are for the physical world, while the laws of the dream world are for the dream world. Keep them separate. Unless you do, you're likely to blunder into some terrible mistakes.

For example, let's say someone in your dream expresses ardent love for you. You take that for his true feelings in the physical world. He may not be aware of them yet and will consider your sudden friendliness pushy. He'll back right off, afraid of you. Actually he's afraid of something he wasn't prepared for—your love.

In this case, play it cool. Feel out the situation a little at a time. Test the waters. Also be ready to accept the fact that this relationship will never develop. Here again, the realities of the dream world may not be suitable for the physical world.

Study your dreams. You'll learn what your dreams mean to your physical life with the Mahanta's help. You keep in touch with him by doing the Spiritual Exercises of ECK.

You may not remember the inner experience exactly as it happened. The dream censor is responsible for that.

Dream Travel and Soul Travel

What is the difference between dream travel and Soul Travel?

It's like watching a video of someone playing in a warm, sunny pool of water or swimming in that pool yourself.

The video shows the sun upon the waters. But if you are in the pool itself, you feel the sunbeams warm your arms and body. The video shows someone else splashing, but in real life you feel the soft kiss of droplets wash over your face and hair.

Do you see? It's like that.

Yet a Soul Travel experience is more real than even a splash in the pool. Soul Travel makes every color around you, every touch, every scent of a flower, every birdsong or tinkling bell seem as if their very atoms have taken on a life of their own.

You feel as if life itself were hugging and kissing you. And blessing you.

Hard as one tries, it's beyond the art of human language to tell the whole story about Soul Travel. But a dream is just a dream. It's like something happening to us at arm's length.

Soul Travel is the real thing.

The reason Soul Travel is so full of life is that in the Soul body we rise in consciousness. We are closer to the full awareness of ECK, the Divine Spirit.

ECK Masters in Dreams

Why do we have to call on the ECK Masters to have good dreams? Do some ECK Masters bring us bad dreams?

Actually, you don't *have to* call on anyone. The ECK Masters are like good teachers you love, so you would *want* to call on them. Otherwise don't.

An ECK Master, like a good teacher, will teach you the lessons most able to help you lead a happy and useful spiritual life. A good dream, then, is helping you grow stronger, wiser, and more full of love.

Then what are bad dreams for?

Children often have nightmares until the age of six or eight, and sometimes longer. Grown-ups do too, though not so often as a rule. But why bad dreams for good people?

A bad dream is generally a memory of a past life. It may include experiences of mistreatment, suffering, and even death. Some of us even have dreams of being born, which can give a feeling of suffocation. These experiences are part of everyone. Children still remember bits and pieces of past lives, and these bad dreams are a part of them.

Bad dreams are old fears.

Having a bad dream is like airing out a musty room in spring. You need to face that old fear until it loses its grip, for only then can you be free to live this life to its fullest.

So good and bad dreams both hold spiritual lessons.

An ECK Master will teach you the lessons most able to help you lead a happy and useful spiritual life.

Protection in Dreams

Once in a while in a dream I confront wild beasts like a panther or wild dogs. Tough situations, but I get control. When I wake up, I ask myself, Why didn't I call upon the Inner Master for help? *Do we always have to ask for and rely on the Mahanta in situations like these? Good sign or bad sign spiritually?*

Also, are psychic attacks always openings that we have made in some way to the psychic forces? Or could they also be allowed in some cases as part of our spiritual training, for testing our spiritual resistance?

Let's start with your dreams.

The particular animal that appears in a dream may carry a less-than-obvious significance at first glance. A book that some find helpful is *Medicine Cards* by Jamie Sams and David Carson, both Native Americans. It is published by St. Martin's Press of New York City.

In this case, wild dogs would represent loyalty that tends to run loose. A panther relates to leadership. If such dreams occur within a few days, weeks, or months of each other, you can be sure that Soul is trying to deliver an important message to your waking consciousness. The mind as censor, however, tries to distort and obscure the original message. So Soul employs images of, say, wild dogs or a panther to slip by this censor. It hopes you catch the intended meaning.

So the Inner Master has given Soul (you) an instruction on how to bolster your leadership skills. The lesson is to examine your spiritual skills and look for ways to keep them consistent and not run wild.

In regard to psychic attacks—

Lots of outer influences can open the doors to them. One who has a solid spiritual foundation in ECK is usually immune to ordinary invasions of personal space by black magicians.

But illness can also open the door to susceptibility. For example, a violent fever can put one out of his head on a short-term basis. Long term, however, Alzheimer's disease may cause memory loss

In the case of dreams and psychic attacks, the Master is there to help if your own efforts need a hand.

and sometimes even open the door to psychic attacks. Yet Soul, the essence of all humans, rests above the fray in peace. It knows that the human instrument is rendered weak by an illness.

In the case of dreams and psychic attacks, the Master is there to help if your own efforts need a hand.

Dance of Soul

I had a lucid dream where I was dancing through the ethers with thousands of Souls, all being drawn to a central point. I was full of joy, knowing that no matter what we do in this world, we are always going to be drawn back to this central point.

A very spiritual dream. It's the dance of Soul for God. The joy is in meeting the true Master and having the true love of God.

I have seen people who have come to an Eckankar seminar and begin crying for no reason. Inwardly, as Soul, they have heard the Voice of God. And God has said, "I love you because you are a part of me, and I am calling you home."

It's a personal experience so strong it changes that person's life. It fills your heart with joy.

It's a personal experience so strong it changes that person's life. At that point he is no longer the same again. Few of his friends and acquaintances can understand what major turning point occurred to him at that point. It's just beyond words. But it is life changing.

Sometimes the love is so strong it's really incredible. It fills your heart with joy. It cleanses the heart, it purifies it; and it gives the person a readiness to accept more of God's love.

This is the secret of the inner teachings.

Difference between
Pretending and Imagination

The other night as I put my five-year-old son to bed, we sang HU together as a love song to God. He had a little cold, so we created a blue "HU bubble" to go over his bed and protect him. We also created a little blue "HU pill" to go inside him to help make him feel better.

It was then he asked me, "Dad, what is the difference between pretending and imagination?" I was floored; I didn't expect this type of question until he was at least ten.

So I said that in the morning we would look in the dictionary. Then we would write a letter to you to ask what the difference is between pretending and the imagination.

In this case, imagination and pretending are much the same thing. Pretending wakes up your imagination, which sees real things, both visible and those yet not seen. So pretending is important. It's step one. Imagination is the second step.

When you pretend, your trust awakens your imagination to make it so.

When you pretend to create a blue HU bubble to go over your bed, your trust in the Mahanta, the Inner Master, awakens your imagination to make it so.

The same is true when you pretend and create a little blue HU pill to go inside you and make you feel better from a cold.

So pretending and imagination are nearly the same thing here. But, in fact, pretending is an important step of make-believe. Imagination, then, is the real thing.

Who Makes the Dream?

I just read about the Dream Master in my ECK youth discourse. Who makes the dream—you, or me, or both of us?

Thank you for a very good question. It is one that many have not thought about. They think the Mahanta would just come to you whenever he pleases.

But that is not so. The spiritual law won't let him, because your state of consciousness is like your home. He would not think of coming into it unless you invite him in.

So, how does a dream with the Mahanta happen?

Many lives ago, you became tired of life, and you called to God to show you the way to your home in heaven.

In answer to your call, Sugmad (God) sent the Mahanta to show you the way to your true home.

He has never left you.

Your state of consciousness is like your home. The Mahanta would not think of coming into it unless you invite him in.

Reality of Inner Experiences

When I go into my dreams and have an experience with the Mahanta, what should I say to him?

You'll know exactly what to say.

Who is your best friend at school? Is it hard to speak to a friend, your parents, or a brother or sister? Of course not. Talking with Wah Z (my spiritual name as the Inner Master) is the same thing.

By the time you meet Wah Z, you will know him as a dear friend of old. This is not your first lifetime, you know. Like everyone else, you've spent so many lifetimes bumping around in spiritual darkness.

Say you're in your home and the electricity goes off. Dark, scary, and lonesome? You bet.

But then you see the bobbing light of a flashlight coming from somewhere, cutting through the curtain of darkness. How do you feel? You get a sudden feeling of relief. Someone's bringing a light.

The Mahanta brings you a light too.

One other point to keep in mind: As above, so below. It means that everything first happens above, on one of the higher spiritual planes: Astral, Causal, etc. So if you're in an ECK family and know of the Mahanta, you've earned the right to meet him.

Now it's simply a matter of remembering. The surest way is by doing one of the many Spiritual Exercises of ECK.

Now it's simply a matter of remembering.

The surest way to remember what happens when we see each other in the dream worlds is by doing one of the many Spiritual Exercises of ECK.

Yes, we know each other and have for a long time. Long before you came to this world.

Friends help each other, or what are friends for? Call on Wah Z anytime. OK?

Doing the Right Thing

I am an ECKist, and I go to a Catholic school. Every Friday we go to church, and I was wondering if I should take communion or not.

Also, instead of hearing things during contemplation, I've been seeing birds—all different kinds—in mesquite trees. I do not know where I am. I have also been seeing a man in my dreams. He was wearing a white suit and a black sombrero. I asked him his name. He said it was Darma. What does that mean?

By now school has started, and you probably know how to handle the problem of whether or not to take communion with the Catholics at your school. If everyone else at your school is a Catholic and takes communion, you'll find it easier to get along by taking it too. It won't hurt you spiritually, so don't worry about that. Communion has no power for people of another religion.

The birds in your contemplation are a very good sign. They sing Sugmad's music to you. The song of birds is one of the many sounds of ECK, the Voice of God. The man in white whose name is Darma (dharma) is also a very spiritual sign from the Mahanta. Dharma means doing the right thing.

The Catholic school should help you learn a good moral and ethical code. Enjoy school and the friends you make there.

The man in white whose name is Darma (dharma) is a very spiritual sign. Dharma means doing the right thing.

Remembering a Dream Adventure

In a dream, a friend gave me a gray crown that did not shine. When I put it on, a bluish-purple crystal hung over my Spiritual Eye, and the crown made my head feel as if it had a glass top. I felt really happy and did not want to take the crown off, but I had to give it back to the owner.

The next day at school, I kept touching my head because it felt like the crown was still there. Can you tell me what this experience means?

The Mahanta let you remember a trip to the Etheric Plane. It's the top part of the Mental Plane. The color blue means the Mental Plane; purple or violet means the Etheric Plane.

What is the gray crown?

The crown means the Spiritual Exercises of ECK. The gray color means that by themselves they are neutral, of no value unless put to their proper use. So you put the crown on your head, where it belonged. Then your spiritual awareness opened, like a glass top on the crown of your head.

A feeling of happiness is a sign of an important spiritual dream. That's why you felt happy at school the next day.

The owner of the crown is the Mahanta. He took it back to polish up for the next time you're ready for another high spiritual dream. So keep doing your spiritual exercises.

A feeling of happiness is a sign of an important spiritual dream.

Snakes in Dreams

In this lifetime, snakes have been a real fear of mine from childhood on. Yet I know that the snake symbol need not be a negative one. I have had three dreams of large snakes during my years in Eckankar. In the first dream, I felt the snake belonged to me, and I had no fear. In the second dream, my husband brought the snake to me to show it wouldn't harm me. I was so afraid that I woke up.

Here is the most recent dream: I walk into a room, and a large snake comes over to me trying to get as close to me as it can, slithering up the right side of my body. I am unafraid and ask the Mahanta, who is also there, "Does it belong to me?" The answer is yes.

Next scene: Looking into an adjacent room, I can see the snake curled up and asleep. At my feet is a pile of wiggling, newborn snakes. I ask the Mahanta, "Are they mine?" The answer is yes.

Would you help me understand the meanings?

A snake in dreams means a spiritual transformation. Not so oddly, the greatest fear among people is that of snakes. People are often afraid of deep changes, especially those of a spiritual nature.

But notice that a snake sheds its skin. It drops the old covering so it can appear in a fresh, new one.

The appearance of a snake in your dreams is a test of your faith and obedience in ECK. How much do you trust the love of God? (Still, here in the physical world few of us would be so foolhardy as to climb into a pit of vipers, yet there are some who manage the feat quite successfully.)

All the little snakes mean the offshoots, or effects, of shedding your old state of consciousness and taking on a new, more refined one. These offspring of a greater consciousness are living with more love and service to others.

In other words, if you're greater inside, it can't help but show outside.

The snake, then, is the birthright of your own unfolding state of awareness, which centers in the inner and outer initiations of ECK.

Your new state of consciousness is like the snake curled up asleep in an adjacent room (a higher state of being away from earth). Yet the demonstrations of it do appear on earth as many small acts of love and kindness to others.

A snake is a good dream symbol, a very spiritual one.

A snake in dreams means a spiritual transformation. A snake sheds its old covering so it can appear in a fresh, new one.

Why Do People Have Bad Dreams?

Why do some people have bad dreams?

Your question is one that bothers many people today. So let's have a look at it.

First on the list of reasons for bad dreams are frightening TV shows and violent computer games.

Especially in the evening before bedtime. They tell a lot. One who indulges in them is falling into a lower state of consciousness.

And where do you suppose he dream travels? To the lower Astral Plane. So, do pleasant things before bedtime. It will clear up many bad dreams.

Second, bad dreams may come from poor nutrition. This can be from not eating the right foods or eating the wrong ones. Too much sugar is a problem, but so are preservatives in food, like monosodium glutamate (MSG). It's used in Chinese food and much else. Both sugar and preservatives fray our nerves. So let's avoid them.

Third, toxins around us can also cause bad dreams. Two common ones are mercury and lead.

The biggest source of mercury pollution comes in communities that burn coal to produce electricity. The burning causes mercury to get into the air, and there's no way to avoid it. Some seafoods, too, are a source of mercury. Ours is a polluted planet, but we all do the best we can.

Toxins are hard to remove from our bodies. There are often doctors of alternative medicine in larger communities who can help us.

So start with reason number one. If you do your part, it'll be easier for me to help you enjoy more pleasant sleep. And sweet dreams!

Do pleasant things before bedtime. It will clear up many bad dreams.

Do Animals Dream?

Do animals have bad dreams? Do they have nightmares with evil entities? If so, do they also sing HU to make them go away?

You must love animals a great deal to have such a good understanding of them. Cats, for example, are much like us in regard to dreams and often give signs of their dreaming.

When a cat's tail twitches, it is likely stalking prey. That is usually a good dream. Its legs moving, as if it is running, can mean the cat is chasing something, or something is chasing it.

Many animals do dream, and their dreams may be good or bad, like people's.

For people, an evil entity often appears as a horribly disfigured entity. It may also look like a normal person, but with an evil look upon its face to send chills along the spine. Or there may rise a disgusting smell.

Cats, in particular, are unusually sensitive to the same entities that frighten people. They can actually see the entities and may announce their presence by arching their backs while staring at some point, say, on a wall. They may likewise hiss. Again, they may show a great reluctance to be in a certain room.

For the most part, only animals in the homes of ECK chelas know of the HU and Its ability to drive away annoying spirits.

Many animals do dream, and their dreams may be good or bad, like people's.

Voices in Dreams

Sometimes I hear a voice, usually male but sometimes female, yell my name. This is usually in the dream state, and it is so loud that it wakes me up. Sometimes it will happen during the day as well. All that is said is my name very loud, as if someone were trying to warn me about something. I always check inwardly to see if there is something I should be aware of, but I can never figure out what the message is. What is the message, and who is giving it?

A spiritual wake-up call is trying to get you to

look at some part of your life that is taken for granted. So look closely at yourself. The voice is an echo of Soul using a human voice to reach your range of hearing. Soul is inspired by the Mahanta, of course. You are an ECK initiate.

Start with a careful examination of your health. It is the usual place for any imbalance of the emotional and mental bodies to appear.

If your health is OK, then look to other areas of your life that could use an update. Sometimes it may mean taking another look at your work, family, friends, free time, and the like.

The voice is simply saying, "It's time to make some changes." Hearing it speak is a divine blessing.

A spiritual wake-up call is trying to get you to look at some part of your life taken for granted.

Symbols in Dreams Are Gifts

I had a dream which has me puzzled. I saw a large, light brown dog. He was somehow fixed in time; he did not move. I saw that his feet, from the ankle downward, did not exist. I felt so pained at this that I started to sing HU. As soon as I sang HU, there were four little white puppies where the large dog should have had its four feet. The dog with no feet disappeared at the same time. Now there were only those four puppies, resting in the green grass with their white mother nearby. All five of them were resting. This scene was so clear. What does it mean?

Clear brown is a good color often associated with someone in business. In your dream, however, it takes on a broader context of material concerns.

A dog stands for loyalty. So a brown dog means a loyalty to materialism that could immobilize one spiritually. Unless, of course, the brown dog's feet are four little white (signifying spiritual purity) puppies.

Four means a foundation or stability. A brown dog with four of its feet missing signifies the frozen or fixed state of a material consciousness. It won't go anywhere.

Yet once the four white puppies take the place of the missing feet, the potential for spiritual growth is magnified four times four. There is one puppy each to represent the Physical, Astral, Causal, and Mental bodies. All these bodies are offspring of Soul, pictured here as the white mother dog. Soul nourishes these four main areas within you.

That all five are resting shows a natural balance in your life. You have a good spiritual foundation now.

This dream is the Mahanta's gift of the ECK-Vidya, the ancient science of prophecy. It's an insight into your present state of consciousness. A highly spiritual dream.

Dreams of Spiritual Insight

I had the following dream one month after first being appointed to an ECK leadership position in my region. This dream experience has come to my attention several times over these past years. I would appreciate your thoughts on it.

I was in a room in a solid and secure house. The room had two windows opposite each other. Looking out one window, I saw a stark, rocky area. A strong wind was blowing, and there was just one stubby tree with no leaves or branches. Beyond there was nothing, just space. Then four or five black birds, like large crows or ravens, landed on the tree. The birds had great difficulty holding on in the strong wind. Their feathers were ruffled, but they all stayed on the tree. Then a white mountain goat walked leisurely past the tree and came close to the window. He was

The four white puppies are offspring of Soul, pictured here as the white mother dog. All five resting shows a natural balance in your life.

not bothered by the strong wind and seemed comfortable in his world.

Walking across the room to the other window I saw a calm, almost meadowlike, snow-covered landscape with some trees and shrubs. A number of small animals were walking, running, or jumping about enjoying themselves, not bothered by the snow. This ended the dream experience.

Your dream is a very spiritual one.

The room reflects your solid and secure state of consciousness. The two windows mean the two viewpoints you need as a key ECK leader in working with and living among members of the ECK community. (I'll explain the rest after treating the particular things you saw outside the two windows.)

The landscape outside the first window shows the thankless task that faces ECKists who volunteer their services for ECK. It's a stark, rocky area. It seems the wind of adversity is always blowing. The single stubby tree is the pure truth of ECK. The space beyond is the limitless reach of creation.

Now, the large black birds are chelas (spiritual students) who land upon the truth and seize it with the claws of the mind. The strong wind is not really adversity, but the ECK. It's the Wind of God. Though ruffled by each gust, they nevertheless hang on gamely to the Tree of Life, which speaks well for them.

Yet there's a better way.

Along comes the white mountain goat. Notice the white coat of spiritual purity. He walks leisurely past the tree. The goat's four feet are solidly planted on the ground, so he is relaxed. That is a symbol of the one chela in maybe four or five who is a heart,

The strong wind is not really adversity, but the ECK. It's the Wind of God.

not mind, person. He's comfortable with himself and the ECK. Naturally, this calmness conveys itself to others.

Then he approaches the window. This signifies your viewpoint. It also suggests you look for other sure-footed, openhearted chelas to help you in your missionary work for the Mahanta, the Living ECK Master.

The second window shows the paradise that other chelas choose to live in: no duties, no responsibilities. Just the idle play of Souls, as in heaven before the Sugmad (God) sent such Souls into these lower worlds for experience. In time, they will tire of play and look to be of more service to God, others, and themselves.

Your dream is a very good spiritual insight into how things really are.

Your dream is good spiritual insight into how things really are.

The Spiritual Exercises of ECK push back the prison of the human consciousness and let in the Light and Sound of God.

4
YOUR
SPIRITUAL TOOLBOX

ow can the Spiritual Exercises of ECK help me live in the moment? What does it really mean to live in the moment?

The basis of the ECK teachings is experience. All that we can ever know depends upon either our own experiences or those of others.

But experience is far from being a spiritual cure-all. Much of it is learning the same old thing over and over again, because we don't accept prior lessons into our state of consciousness. And so, old lessons repeat. This refusal or inability to learn is what karma and reincarnation are all about.

So an ECKist does not want to spin his wheels. Nor should he ever have to.

Living in the moment means integrating the lessons of yesterday into the actions of today. Yes, an ECKist does make plans. He makes plans to arrange his affairs so they run as smoothly as possible. He allots his time to activities which

Living in the moment means integrating the lessons of yesterday into the actions of today.

benefit him and others.

Now, how does he avoid getting sucked into the whirlpool that catches the unwary traveler and brings on destruction?

Simple. He practices the Spiritual Exercises of ECK each day. He sings a holy name of God or the ECK while he is up and about. These are the right actions. They push back the prison of the human consciousness and let in the Light and Sound of God. The spiritual exercises prepare a warm and friendly place in the heart for the Mahanta to stay.

Living in the moment, then, depends upon experience taken to heart in the right way.

Much of the experience of people on the wheel of death and rebirth is *unconscious* experience. So they run in a circle. The Spiritual Exercises of ECK, however, lead to *conscious* experience. They go in the most direct way to Sugmad (God) in the Ocean of Love and Mercy.

Help with Solving Problems

How do you help people solve problems? If someone is feeling scared or hurt inside, how do you help them, and how can you listen to so many?

There are two ways to help people solve a problem.

Let's look at your first question. There are two ways to help people solve a problem: do it for them, or let them do most or all of it alone.

Which way do you think gives them more experience to care for themselves, to survive? And which way do you think builds the most confidence?

The second way, of course.

So the Mahanta, the Living ECK Master prefers to use the second method, unless there is a great, immediate need to help someone who is unable to do it alone. Either way, however, is an ECK miracle.

Second question . . .

The Master helps people overcome fear by showing them a way to solve or lessen their fearful situation. He gives hope. He grants ideas. He may send others to offer aid. He may also remove a threat with an out-and-out miracle.

And how to help those who hurt inside? He brings love. It comes to fill a heart in its darkest hour. Or, again, he may appear in a dream to show the karmic reason for the pain.

To see the root of a problem is often all it takes to make a hurt fly away.

And, last, how does the Master listen to so many? It's all about the Rod of ECK Power. It makes the Master one with the Holy Spirit, so he has all Its qualities, like the ability to be anywhere and everywhere there is a spiritual need.

To see the root of a problem is often all it takes to make a hurt fly away.

Our Talents and Pride

Do we have some sort of obligation to use our talents, and is pride an obstacle on our way to mastership?

Yes and yes.

As to the first: any obligation is to you yourself, not to another.

A talent is a divine gift. You developed it in one or more past lives, taking a stick on the nose from a demanding authority when your efforts fell short of his needs. That discipline shaped you. A bundle of lessons like that lifted you to a higher state of consciousness, as did many, many others. It was so you could move on spiritually.

Love and safeguard your most prized talents. They helped you become who you are today.

Of course, if you are rich in talents, develop and add to a select few you love above the rest. Choose well. The fact is, we can't do everything in this lifetime. Put your heart into the few. Then your projects will flourish in a natural way. There will surely be tasks not to our liking. Let your talents excel in their completion too.

Your joys, moreover, let you glide through the forest of necessary but unwelcome tasks. Joys are a balance.

And pride? It is of two clashing kinds: the good and the ugly.

On the plus side there is pride in a good thing done well. It makes you glow all around. Small things count, like a good grade on a test you studied for. Maybe a birthday card you created for your mother or dad out of love. It can include cleaning up your room.

The signs of an ugly pride? How about stealing the credit for another's achievements, or comparing your grace to someone's pratfalls, or holding your nose above others?

Such pride comes before a fall.

Put your heart into the talents you love. Then your projects will flourish in a natural way.

Unwinding Attachment

I find myself in an awkward situation. Leaders I admire are using so-called love and their spiritual status to control me.

The control is so subtle, it is hard to see. I am to believe their spiritual experiences, or connection, is greater than mine so I should listen to them and do things the way they want me to. Love is given, but it comes with strings attached.

So how do I know when someone is trying to manipulate my energy and attention for their gain? And once I really know, as Soul, that this is happening, how do I deal with it?

By writing down this question so clearly, it shows that you, as Soul, already know that someone is trying to manipulate your energy and attention for their gain.

So let's go to the second question.

In contemplation, ask the Mahanta to show you what *you* are gaining from such an involvement. It couldn't exist without some sort of a mutual benefit. At one time, when you let such people into your personal life, the benefit to both sides was in balance. But now you are on the short end. That's why you're unhappy.

First, try to see what has changed. If the problems weigh more than the benefits, ask the Mahanta to show the best way to unwind your involvement with grace and goodwill. That is the second, most important part.

This is a spiritual lesson in self-responsibility. It will make you stronger. More loving.

This spiritual lesson in self-responsibility will make you stronger. More loving.

Obstacles to God-Realization

What would you say is the greatest obstacle for someone trying to get to God-Realization?

The greatest obstacle to God is usually the person himself.

People, in their experience in life, go through all the ups and downs of everyday living. They get the feeling they learn something, but often, in a single lifetime, they don't learn a whole lot. This is why there's such a need to experience going through many, many lives.

By the time they come to a lifetime where they find ECK, they've had just about every experience you can imagine. Unless, of course, it happens to be one of their first lifetimes in ECK, where people generally leave the path in disappointment and disillusionment, only to come back centuries later.

Fit the Spiritual Exercises to You

When I do my spiritual exercises or sing HU, sometimes I feel like I can't keep going. It's so hard for me to sing for any length of time or to do a full spiritual exercise. Why do I have such a difficult time concentrating, and what can I do about it?

You wrote this question while a student in Spain. The country has a strong Catholic tradition. That centuries-old tradition is like a radio station broadcasting radio waves to all corners of Spain.

Those waves rise from the Astral Plane. They will try to cause interference with the spiritual practices of other religions.

HU will let you ride on top of the negative waves.

So, do more short spiritual exercises. Fit them into a new rhythm of living. Ebb and flow with the psychic currents, but ride on top of them. There's a way to do that. Sing HU but once when there's a need. Let HU fill your heart, though.

HU will let you ride on top of the negative waves.

The time in Spain is a good opportunity to learn flexibility with the Spiritual Exercises of ECK.

Fit the spiritual exercises to you, instead of you to them.

My book *The Spiritual Exercises of ECK* gives dozens of them. The great number are a means of teaching ECK chelas (spiritual students) to be flexible. After all, life flows. So must we. That means in every department of our life.

No, flexibility does not include bending the spiritual laws. Rather, we learn to move around blocks, because life provides a way around them.

Did you ever watch a leaf floating downstream in a brook? It will catch on a twig, then free itself. Then, on with the journey.

My love and thoughts are with you on your journey.

Making Choices

When making important choices that will determine a lot of my life experiences, how can I know I am following my highest inner guidance?

For example, how can I find the career that aligns with my spiritual destiny but provides me with stability and security? Or in choosing a mate, how do I know if the relationship is going to grow into a future of the highest love?

So my question is, How do you really get inner guidance, understand it enough to trust it, and have the discipline to follow it?

If you stay true to your mission in life, which is to become a Co-worker with God, the Holy Spirit and the Mahanta will guide you to the right places in life.

The real question is: How can one keep on track toward that mission? By the faithful practice of the

Did you ever watch a leaf floating downstream in a brook? It will catch on a twig, then free itself. Then, on with the journey.

Spiritual Exercises of ECK.

Now, it helps to understand a few things.

Just because you keep it in mind that life is trying to help you become a Co-worker with God doesn't mean that life will necessarily be easy. That depends upon your spiritual needs.

But know that no government or human establishment can ever deliver on the vain promise to provide people with security from the cradle to the grave. That's not the purpose of life. There is no stability or security on earth. Any doubts? Study history to see how people manage to harm each other in wars, on the streets, and in the courts. That's life.

Few spiritual seekers ever fall into a lifetime career on the first try. Free will plays a major role in our future.

That extends even to choosing a mate. Both people in the relationship must do their best to love and build up their mate. If one or both of them fail at this, the relationship comes to hard times.

To get true inner guidance, give God, the Mahanta, and yourself the purest love. And do your spiritual exercises in the same spirit of love.

Dealing with Distractions

Often I have distractions in life, school, relationships, etc., that make it hard to keep myself disciplined. What advice do you have to help youth keep focused and disciplined with their spiritual exercises? Also, some youth have difficulty just sitting still. Are there active ways to do spiritual exercises?

The whole purpose of distractions is to throw

your attention off the ECK, the Holy Spirit. Discipline is what you came here to learn.

You rightly make the connection between a focused discipline and the spiritual exercises. The exercises are the golden key to a life of meaning and happiness.

Are there active ways to do the spiritual exercises? Sure, a lot of them.

For younger children, say, "Shut your eyes a minute. Imagine there's a piece of white paper in front of you and all the colors you need are beside it. Draw a big flower. Done? OK, now draw a happy face on it. That's the Mahanta. Listen, did he tell you something special?"

Whatever spiritual exercise you create, be sure that it lets the child be an actor in it. The child must have the lead role in the theater of his spiritual exercise.

The ECK teachings, you see, help people on their own path home to God. So each person is the star in his own world.

The spiritual exercises are the golden key to a life of meaning and happiness.

Importance of Soul Travel

Why is it so important in Eckankar to learn Soul Travel?

Soul Travel, in its broader sense, is very important because it deals exclusively with the expansion of spiritual awareness. In other words, people have to, at some time, become aware of who and what they are. This knowledge is also opened to them through dreams, or through some other way—their past lives and the possibilities for the future.

But more important: Soul Travel—which means moving into the higher regions of God, to regions people haven't even been to before—opens them to divine love.

This is more important than any of the other journeys into inner space. Moving into the inner planes through Soul Travel—whether in a very focused or a very broad, expansive manner—opens the heart to divine love. This is what all life is about.

Resistance

Would you say something about the resistance we get from the universe when we are striving to make a big step ahead spiritually or as an ECK leader? How can we deal with it?

The gatekeeper at every portal is a follower of the Kal force. And yet, each of these guardians is also Soul, albeit in a sleep state. The Master loves one and all.

Pure love is the only thing that will ever melt any resistance.

So regardless of the hurdles they place in your path with utmost diligence, they do retain a bit of spiritual hearing and sight. Pure love is the only thing that will ever melt any resistance.

Again, it is all about love, and love alone.

In a practical sense, then, we enlist the help of the most competent allies we can find to unlock the gate of resistance. For example, a certain librarian will not allow an ECK talk in the library. So speak to a senior library official or look for another location. Here's the time to ask around. Maybe the Chamber of Commerce can suggest sites to hold public events, etc.

But whomever you approach, do it with love. Imagine the Mahanta in the room or on the phone with you during a request of some official or other key person.

When the time and place are right, Divine Spirit will open all the gates. You need but seek till you find.

Resistance, you see, is for our own good. It is to give us strength and wisdom by way of experience.

Experience is the only teacher.

Love your teacher.

Keeping My Balance

When I do my spiritual exercises and succeed in rising above the Soul Plane, I cannot bring back any memory of where I have been, but only a sense of joy and happiness.

Then the rush of life takes over, and the situations and problems bring sorrow and pain into my life. The intensity of this seems to be in proportion to the joy and happiness felt before. At this point, the only solace is to chant HU.

I'd like to learn how to keep my state of balance more firm. Could you please comment?

The ECK teachings keep our focus on the spiritual *benefits* of facing life, instead of the all-too-common string of hardships. The mind has a hard time putting an experience from the Soul Plane into human metaphors so they can reach your waking self. The mind feels like a pen without an author.

Yet it is possible to undertake the discipline to recall fragments of journeys into the regions beyond time and space. Start with the following steps.

When you awaken, put in a dream notebook any impression at all that lingers from the night's experience. It can be a single line. For example: "Last night I rose above the Soul Plane. What I do recall is a sense of joy and happiness."

The ECK teachings keep our focus on the spiritual benefits of facing life, instead of the all-too-common string of hardships.

Keep every statement a positive one.

Avoid any thought or mention of the body of knowledge either lost or forgotten. All records must be positive. After all, these records are of journeys into the pure positive worlds of God.

Make it a habit to make some entry in your dream journal after every successful session of contemplation.

Again, the entry may be a single sentence. But date each entry. There could be a dozen entries on a single page (the Law of Economy, you see).

You can remember your spiritual travels. Many others have learned the skill before you, and many more shall learn it still. Spiritual balance comes of this practice.

Happiness

How can we be happy when we have difficult experiences in our life?

Usually we're not happy then. The difficulty takes up all our time and attention. But it's later, when an old relationship, for example, is replaced by a new and better one, that the sunbeam of happiness again finds us.

How do you get by in the dark times? Try to give love to someone, especially then.

Life is a stream of happy and unhappy experiences, because that leads to Soul's purification.

How do you get by in the dark times? Try to give love to someone, especially then.

Being Able to Concentrate

I do not know how to concentrate. When I want to contemplate on a certain subject, I lose control and start thinking of anything. Do you have any suggestions that could help me?

Paul Twitchell, the modern-day founder of Eckankar, once wrote that the mind likes to jump around like a monkey.

First of all, don't worry about it.

Second, entertain your mind during the Spiritual Exercises of ECK. Do an exercise a slightly different way each time. Let the mind play. Remember who is watching your mind play: the real you (Soul). Come to that realization during your spiritual exercise, and you will realize that Soul Itself is calm and doesn't jump around.

It's hard to get the mind absolutely still. But by suddenly knowing that you, the watcher (Soul), are still, the antics of the mind won't upset you anymore.

After all, the mind jumps around to upset you. Does this help you?

Singing HU

HU is the main mantra used in Eckankar. It has also been used in other spiritual traditions in the past. What makes this one-syllable word so powerful?

It's powerful because it's the ancient name for God. It's a name that some of the Eastern religions are aware of, but in the West, it's pretty much an unknown name. And it is much more effective as a love song to God than just the simple Anglo-Saxon word *God*.

HU is ancient. When people come back to ECK, it's the name that they recognize from other lifetimes. When they come back to ECK, they're going to remember. They're going to find help in their lives when using it, when singing it, because it makes a connection all the way back through the earliest

HU is ancient. When people come back to ECK, it's the name they recognize from other lifetimes.

times when people came to this planet. People who reincarnated a long time ago have this unconscious knowledge of it. And the ones who have been here before many times love the sound.

Not Getting in Our Own Way

So what is the key for learning to step aside and not get in the way?

Putting your attention so much upon God through singing HU or some other method, so that God becomes the substance of your life.

When I say this, I do it with some hesitation. When I say *God becomes the substance of your life*, people put together all the wrong messages ever gathered in this life or previous lives. They put it together all wrong. For instance they say, "All right, to love God a lot means to leave my family; it means to go out in the desert somewhere, to go up in the mountains, and to cut myself off from humanity. That is showing my love for God." Nothing could be farther from the truth.

That's why I'm really hesitant about saying that God must become the entire focus of the person's life. What I would suggest instead is to sing this word *HU* or some other name of God. It will lift you into the higher levels of spiritual realization.

To sing this word HU will lift you into the higher levels of spiritual realization.

In God's Time

Sometimes I'm faced with challenges and there is no immediate answer. If this ever happens to you, what specific things do you do to find the next step?

I sit and wait.

However, it is a being still and doing something. That "something" is a constant spiritual exercise in which I'm aware every second of what the ECK is revealing to me inwardly and outwardly about a circumstance.

That does take patience. Sometimes the ECK gives the answer piecemeal over many days, weeks, or months. So patience and discipline are keys to understanding a trying situation.

Quiet Hours

I have been waking in the early morning hours and then been unable to go back to sleep. Is there spiritual significance in this?

The quiet hours of the early morning are most conducive for spiritual communion with the Mahanta. By then, the cares of the previous day have usually subsided, and the concerns of the new day have yet to take hold.

Use this time for a brief spiritual exercise. Often, you'll fall into a light sleep again and in some way receive a spiritual insight or a blessing from the Mahanta.

Being an Effective Channel for God

What do you do so you can still be an effective channel for God when the intensity of the spiritual flow increases enough to cause discomfort?

A good way to balance the spiritual intensity is to get more physical exercise. Of course, be careful if you're badly out of shape. You want to get a medical checkup before doing anything out of the ordinary.

Sometimes the ECK gives the answer piecemeal over many days, weeks, or months. So patience and discipline are keys to understanding a trying situation.

Good health depends upon a balance of your emotions, mind, body, and spiritual side. It's easy to get too mental. The mind generates a lot of power, which can work to the disadvantage of your health unless you get enough physical exercise. Make time for it.

Often, a regular walk in the park is all it takes. Make it a part of your daily schedule. There are a lot of riches in this world, but they mean nothing without health.

Keeping Your Space Clear

I had some strong thoughts and desires. Then I discovered they belonged to others. How do I recognize which thoughts are mine? Do you have any suggestions for keeping my space clear?

It's a part of your spiritual training. No matter what the source of our thoughts and desires, it does matter a lot what we finally do with them. Do we take the high spiritual path or not?

Thoughts and desires are like radio beams, bombarding our minds with hundreds of promptings each hour.

Thoughts and desires are like radio beams. They originate at every imaginable level, bombarding our minds with hundreds of promptings each hour. Our past spiritual experience filters most of them out. Thus, we're not aware of those. But other thoughts and desires are stronger or newer to us. They exist in our consciousness because we haven't fully decided yet whether it would be too spiritually harmful to give in to them.

That's where experience comes in.

To keep your space clear, keep your heart and mind steadfastly on being a Co-worker with God and all that implies in your conduct.

Making Good Changes

Do you have suggestions for how to bring about important changes I want to make in my life?

Old assumptions make us what we are, and those that hold us back from any sort of success are the hardest to recognize and correct. But it can be done. What better use of a lifetime than to learn better ways to come into the rhythm of life.

Tolerance and love of the Divine Self are at the top of the list. We must love our divine nature before we can love anyone else, but, of course, everything is a matter of degree. Slow and easy does it.

What better use of a lifetime than to learn better ways to come into the rhythm of life.

Building Self-Esteem

How do I learn to truly love myself and build self-esteem? I have struggled with self-esteem, weight issues, and a core lack of confidence for many years. Is there a practical tool or spiritual exercise that will help? Plus, what is the spiritual significance of such a barrier?

There is a single reason for the three problems you mentioned. It is simply fear.

We may fear another's rejection.

So we, in fact, line up a bunch of excuses for the occasion when someone does reject us. And yet, we're thus laying the groundwork for future unhappiness too. We gain weight to be unattractive. But in doing so, we also shut the door on possible opportunities to meet people who could bring us happiness.

Poor self-esteem and a lack of self-confidence are, for the most part, the very same problem.

What's at play here? A fear of rejection!

To counter such a possibility, we go halfway to meet any and all rejections before they even get a chance to occur. It is an upside-down way of living. We go to great lengths to make the negative expressions of fear come true. It's no wonder we're unhappy, isn't it?

The question now is, What to do about it?

Fear is your assailant. Love is the antidote.

So fear is your assailant. Love is the antidote. Whenever you become aware of fear trying to throw you back into old, negative patterns, know that Sugmad, the ECK, and the Mahanta do love you. In recognition of this divine love, sweetly sing one of the holy names. This will gradually let you love yourself and build self-esteem.

Creating Your Life

A while ago, I was doing a spiritual exercise that was an extension of the "as if" principle. At the time, I was unhappy with work and relationship issues, and so I began to write in my journal each day about the life I wanted to create for myself.

It changed me completely and helped me focus on particular goals. Within weeks, the experience I had written about in my journal began to manifest.

How do I know, when practicing an exercise of this nature, that I am working in alignment with spiritual law and not infringing on the spiritual freedom of others?

In your first paragraph, the key words are "the life I wanted to create for myself." So was it an upright, honest goal?

Then, in your third paragraph, the key words are "working in alignment with spiritual law and not infringing on the spiritual freedom of others." One could too casually say, Well, are you? But that is exactly your question.

So give room for the ECK, the Mahanta, to determine whether your goal is in keeping with the divine laws.

Phrase your wishes on this order: "If I am ready, let me pass from my present situations into ones more in keeping with a higher state of consciousness." Then hold your wishes lightly in mind. And let whatever will be, be.

Do not overlook an important fact. Your ability to even envision a brighter future is not by chance. This vision alone is saying something that is obvious.

It says you are no longer satisfied with things as they have become. Who or what has changed?

This answer is purposely vague. You must examine these and other such issues honestly in your own heart. Ask the Inner Master's guidance too.

The Golden Rule

You suggest that the best way to make a good decision or to react correctly is to ask the three following questions: Is it true? Is it necessary? Is it kind?

The first two questions appear very easy to me, because the response depends on my opinion or my state of Soul at the moment. But the third is much more delicate because I must, to be honest, put myself in the other person's skin in order to respond in all sincerity.

In this case, should I consider (1) their personality, emotions, ego? or (2) a principle or spiritual law that is important to observe?

The best way to make a good decision or to react correctly is to ask: Is it true? Is it necessary? Is it kind?

Is it kind? Indeed, that question does take special consideration.

You surely will take into account their personality, emotions, and ego. It's the art of diplomacy. That is, the skill of handling affairs and not arousing hostility. It is the use of tact.

Is there a principle or spiritual law that is important to observe?

Yes, there is—the law of love.

This law is easy to apply. Just think of the Golden Rule: Do unto others as you would have them do unto you. The Golden Rule makes it much easier to carry on in your leadership roles and in your personal life.

Blue Star

My mom says the Blue Star is a symbol for the ECK. Is it really a symbol, how do you see it, and what does it mean?

The Blue Star, or Blue Light, is one way the Mahanta often appears to someone. You'll see it in contemplation.

Your mom is right. The Blue Star, or Blue Light, is one way the Mahanta often appears to someone at first. He is one with the ECK. So in the fullest sense the Blue Star, or Blue Light, is the ECK. You'll see it in contemplation.

Of course, the Blue Light *is* real. Looked at like that, it's not a symbol at all—because it is real. A symbol is not the thing itself, just a mental picture made to illustrate it.

To make the difference more clear to you, here's an example: Charles Schulz is a cartoonist. He draws two-dimensional pictures of children, like Charlie Brown, Lucy, and Linus. Let's not forget Snoopy, Charlie Brown's dog.

All these characters are only symbols. They don't even look like real characters.

But we know that the cartoonist's drawings are meant to be seen by his readers as children or dogs, because they somewhat look, talk, or act like them.

A symbol is shorthand for something that is more, something real.

So the symbol of the Blue Light used in the ECK publications is not the ECK (the Holy Spirit) or the Mahanta. It is just a simple reminder of them. A spiritual symbol can inspire someone to become a better, wiser person with more love and compassion for others.

Spirituality in Busy Times

What are the most beneficial ways to do our spiritual exercises during these busy times? Can you comment on the value of spiritual exercises done on the run (while doing other activities) compared with doing only a twenty-minute spiritual exercise?

The Spiritual Exercises of ECK adapt to all situations. That's part of what makes them so relevant for ECKists worldwide who grapple with a wide spectrum of conditions.

The Spiritual Exercises of ECK adapt to all situations.

ECK accommodates all, gives life to all.

Doing the spiritual exercises on the run is an excellent time for them. You benefit from the Mahanta's help and encouragement on the spot, when you most notice and appreciate it.

On the run you are most alive. All your senses are awake, and they lend a heightened awareness of the sea of life flowing around you.

The usual twenty-minute exercise gives you a

chance to sit in peace with a dear and treasured friend. It's like a sit-down lunch with no distractions. Your spiritual meal with the Mahanta lets you savor his company.

So both spiritual exercises are fine.

Even if on-the-run spiritual exercises are a fact of life, put your attention lightly upon the Mahanta at bedtime. Then just go to sleep.

There you have an all-night exercise.

Secret Word

What if, as a child, you forgot your special word for contemplation? How do you find another one? And why are they so important? Isn't HU good enough? Also, what do you do if spiritual exercises just don't work or have the same effect as they used to, or if concentration is nearly impossible for some reason? And why does this happen?

Lots of questions. All are answered elsewhere in the ECK teachings. But here's a short version: *How to find another special word?*

The answer is in your contemplations. In some way, at some time, the Mahanta will give it to you either in a dream, by intuition, or in your waking outer life. Be open to all possible words. Try one new one at a time during each spiritual exercise.

And by all means, flip through *A Cosmic Sea of Words: The ECKANKAR Lexicon* for new ideas. When a word stands out, experiment with it.

Yes, HU is good enough.

All sounds and, indeed, all words derive from it. A special word gives a focus to some particular aspect of your spiritual unfoldment. For example, walking is a good general exercise. But if you'd like

A special word gives a focus to some aspect of your spiritual unfoldment.

to develop more grace, a rhythmic dance would serve you better.

No spiritual exercise will always work the way it used to.

Things change. After all, isn't change the very nature of life? Nothing is ever the same. A lesson learned early or late in the ECK teachings is that Soul can go in one of three ways in any stage of Its spiritual unfoldment. It can move forward, backward, or stand still. That's it.

Why is concentration nearly impossible at times?

Here individuals must look at their own discipline. The mind is a restless creation, like a disobedient or destructive child. Soul, like a good parent, must bring it into line. And the sooner the better. The longer a bad habit is allowed free rein, the more unruly it becomes.

Your questions are good ones. I hope these answers give you a better spiritual understanding.

Fill Your Life with Love

How can we help new members as well as long-time ECKists fill their life with the Mahanta so that he becomes part of their everyday life?

You could give them a walk-around spiritual exercise to help meet daily problems.

It's this: When in doubt about the best course of action to handle any of the many perplexities that crop up during the waking hours, ask yourself, *What would Wah Z (Z or Harji) do?*

Use one of my spiritual names. They are more personal in this case than my title, the Mahanta, the Living ECK Master.

A walk-around spiritual exercise to help meet daily problems: When in doubt about the best course of action, ask yourself, What would Wah Z do?

For you see, what draws a chela (spiritual student) closer to the Master is a daily practice of the Spiritual Exercises of ECK. This exercise accomplishes this goal at the heart, rather than the mind, level.

Of course, it's up to the ECKists to do any spiritual exercise. Yet it will bring them into the grace of Sugmad's (God's) love better than anything else you could suggest.

Getting Answers

I find it hard to ask questions during contemplation and then listen for answers. Can you tell me the best way to listen and get answers without my mind going to other places, causing distraction?

The answers may not come during contemplation. Often they come later in the day or week. But they do come.

Your mind, like the minds of many others, likes to jump around. It's unable to focus on one thing. The Mahanta does give you answers in contemplation, but they get lost in a sea of other answers, creations of your mind.

But read on. There is a way to overcome the play of mind.

Once, in a grocery store, I complimented the woman at the checkout stand on how fast she could identify the many different greens and vegetables in plastic bags and then punch the right codes into the computer. She was as fast as an automatic scanner. She was modest about her skills.

"Practice and repetition," she said. "Practice and repetition."

The answers may not come during contemplation. Often they come later in the day or week. But they do come.

It's the same with the Spiritual Exercises of ECK. It takes practice and repetition. Before long, the mind will behave and stop acting like a spoiled child, for that's what it is. It's used to having its own way.

But if you practice the spiritual exercises on a regular schedule, like a meal, you'll get the inner nourishment you seek.

Staying in Line with the ECK

While doing my spiritual exercises, I sometimes put myself on the Soul Plane and look down. The Soul Plane, to me, looks like a mirror of Light all around. Other times it is like seeing all around this planet from outside.

Then I try to project on the planes above. A few times I have seen just light—white, yellow, and gold. I look for experiences, but it seems that outside time and space there are only feelings. When I come back, I feel light and detached, which is really great.

I'm looking for a yardstick to see if I'm in line with the ECK. Could you please comment on this?

Everyone and everything is in its rightful place at this moment or they wouldn't be there.

You have a good spiritual yardstick. You are certainly in line with the ECK. Now, to find a way to help others find their own true yardsticks through the ECK teachings too.

Outside of time and space there are only perceptions. It's hard to find the right word to describe reality on the Soul Plane and above, but it is "perception." "Feelings" comes closest, but it's of the Astral Plane, the place of emotions, of feelings.

If you practice the spiritual exercises on a regular schedule, like a meal, you'll get the inner nourishment you seek.

The benefits of the Soul Plane and beyond are truly that of a light and detached state. If only we could pass that saving knowledge on to others who are seeking it but haven't found it.

Someone had the goodness to light your way. A grateful Soul will do as much for others.

Healing means doing something in a new way to regain health. The old ways are put on the shelf as attempts begin to restore the individual's vitality.

5
HEALTH
AND HEALING

I know there are innumerable opportunities daily for spiritual growth. Many are suffering. Is healing intimately connected with spiritual growth? Is there an easier way to grow?

Don't we wish?

The greatest unfoldment occurs when our feet are put to the fire. What is ill health? It's the result of a deliberate or else an unconscious violation of laws for a period of time. This ignorance of karmic law reflects imperfection. Healing, then, means doing something in a new way to regain health. The old ways, at least for the moment, are put on the shelf as attempts begin to restore the individual's vitality.

Healing means doing something different, if not new.

Soul in the lower worlds is in an imperfect state, a sort of sickness, if you will. It gets into a rut of pleasure, with no regard for consequences, and that attitude finds quick support from an army of habits.

Ill health is the result of a deliberate or else unconscious violation of laws for a period of time.

These habits spin from the five perversions of the mind. They're our old friends greed, lust, anger, vanity, and undue attachment to material things.

So these habits have us put things into and upon and to our bodies that cause long-term harm. These habits also infest our minds and thus govern our emotions.

Habits are tough characters. They pay little mind to reason or persuasive arguments. In protest, then, our bodies, like an overloaded donkey, sit down. That's illness.

So you see, there is no better way to unfold in spiritual terms than by meeting ourselves.

In fact, it's the only way.

For all its discomfort and the apparently random strings of cause and effect, this old world is a masterpiece of design. It's for the weak to become stronger. It's the place to learn all about God's love and how it's so much larger than all our petty bits of self-interest gathered into one bundle—our human body.

There is no better way to unfold in spiritual terms than by meeting ourselves.

Miracles

What is a miracle? How do we open our consciousness to them all the time?

A dictionary might say that a miracle is an event that shows God's intervention in a human crisis. That's only half of it.

What if a tragedy occurs and God did not step in to avert it? No miracle? Sometimes there is, but the miracle is in how the victim responds spiritually to the tragedy. No one is immune from troubles; this is earth, you must remember.

Often, one needs to look into a past life. Ask the

Mahanta to show you in some way the reason for the distressful event—and your past deeds that brought on the present troubles. Things happen to let us grow.

Stay close to the Mahanta (do your spiritual exercises) and your consciousness will naturally open to see the miracles around you every day.

The True Healer

How do you heal people?

The true healer is the ECK, Divine Spirit. When a healing takes place, it is through the power of the ECK. I don't take credit myself.

This question raises another: If one person is healed of a problem, why not all people?

The reason is that a healing depends a lot upon one's opening his heart to love. When some people need a healing, they think only about their love for the Mahanta. They love him more than their illness. A miracle then occurs.

A healing depends a lot upon one's opening his heart to love.

Even more important, they are willing not to have a healing, because they know that their illness is for a reason. It is helping them grow spiritually.

Helping Others to Heal Yourself

I am sixty-seven years old, not in the best of health, and I am very depressed. Five months ago, I lost my husband after forty-six years of marriage. We had eight children and a very full life together.

I am so lost and just can't seem to function. I am a Catholic and always have been strong in my faith in God, but I do not know how to cope anymore. My daughter is an ECKist and feels you can be of some help for me.

Thank you for your letter. No one else can fully understand the loss of a husband of forty-six years, but my love and concern are with you in your present state of unhappiness.

If your health allows, try to help other people in some way as a volunteer. You *must* do that to fill the awful loneliness inside you. Have young children you like near you. Some children can be a trial to be around, so be with a loving, giving child (as a babysitter, perhaps).

Sometimes it just helps to *listen* to others who need a friendly ear. Is there some sort of volunteer work you can do for your church? You need to help others again, even as you were there for your husband.

I feel so helpless in the face of your grief and loss, because there is no easy way to ever replace someone who's become so dear to us as life itself. But if you can find a way to help others, at least a little of your sorrow will lift and the love of God will find you.

If you can find a way to help others, at least a little of your sorrow will lift and the love of God will find you.

Dark Night of Soul

This past weekend I visited an ECKist in his midforties with terminal cancer. He is not concerned with the cancer as much as his apparent loss of connection with Divine Spirit. Is it possible for someone to "lose" their connection with the ECK or do they allow their connection to be diminished through their circumstances? What advice can I give this person?

The dark night of Soul is an intrinsic part of the spiritual day. Thus the old saying that it is darkest before the dawn.

A person in a dark night of Soul most appreciates the gift of quiet understanding. He'd like a listening ear, not advice. He knows the end is near. He also knows that no earth-given advice or aid can erase the mortal human condition.

So the best you can do is to love him and listen.

The dark night of Soul will then be a less lonely time, for the Master's love and assurance will appear and dispel his fear.

He's OK.

A person in a dark night of Soul most appreciates the gift of quiet understanding.

How to Eat Right

I'm having trouble with eating junk food. I eat it because I have cravings. Then I feel bad and get sick. What can I do to help myself stop?

Cravings often develop into destructive habits, as in your case. There's no easy way to break a bad habit.

But first try to find the reasons for your cravings. Is your body getting enough good nutrition? Chances are it isn't, if you're filling up on junk food. Maybe your parents can help find a dietitian to develop a good diet for you. But let's be honest; that's probably not going to work. Habits are very hard to break.

Sometimes we eat because we feel we're not getting enough love. This stage can occur a lot of times in life. For example, now you're growing up. You're leaving the age of a young child, who gets most things done for it by parents, and are moving into a time of life where they (and everyone else) expect you to care more for yourself. Parents dress and undress babies and young children, and put away their clothes, and keep their room in order. As you get older now, do those things for yourself.

That last sentence gets to the heart of overeating due to feelings of not getting enough love. To get love, you must first give love—as an *older* child. A way to give love is by doing things for yourself. That's loving yourself.

So, to get love, you must first give love. For others to love you, you must be lovable. Start by loving yourself. How? You begin to put away your clothes and keep your room in order.

Love yourself first and other people will too.

Here's the reason it's so important to love yourself in the first place: Others will only love you if you learn to love yourself first. To get love, give love. Love yourself first and other people will too.

There are about ten more things to say about getting over bad habits, but I'll tell them to you in your dreams. Pay attention.

Your Diet and Your Spiritual Growth

How important is diet to spirituality?

Not important at all, IF . . . (Note the big *if*.)

If the foods in your diet let you feel and act with love, charity, and wisdom, then diet makes no difference at all to your spirituality.

But if a certain food, like a caffeine-loaded soft drink, makes you edgy or short-tempered, then you are sure to make some negative karma for yourself. That, of course, will hold you back spiritually.

Or if you like foods saturated with fat, like too many pizzas or hamburgers, and they let you put on too much weight. No problem spiritually if you're happy with the few extra pounds. A problem occurs, though, if the added weight upsets you. Do you then have a low opinion of yourself? If so, your attitude would hold you back spiritually.

So eat and drink what you please. If you find that some food or beverage is bringing you unhappiness or sickness, ask the Mahanta to help you control it.

Spiritual Effect of Bad Habits

What do bad habits like smoking, drinking, etc., do to our spiritual bodies? Does this halt our spiritual advancement?

Yes. It riddles your aura with holes, to allow negative currents in. It destroys good judgment.

Accepting Your Body

Last year I struggled my way through anorexia. I thought that I was fully over it until just recently when I began to throw up my food. I am too scared to tell anyone and do not want to become bulimic.

How can I just accept my body and stop the eating disorders altogether?

To make a long answer short, I suggest you read *The Healing Power of Illness: The Meaning of Symptoms and How to Interpret Them* by Thorwald Dethlefsen and Rudiger Dahlke, MD. Look in the index for anorexia nervosa.

This book takes a hard look at the condition.

Building Blocks to Health

I've recently started studying yoga, and I love the physical and mental benefits that I receive from

If the added weight upsets you, do you then have a low opinion of yourself? If so, your attitude would hold you back spiritually.

practicing it, but I know that many use yoga for spiritual upliftment as well. Is there any conflict with practicing the physical elements of yoga and growing spiritually on the path of ECK?

There is no conflict.

Yoga offers definite benefits in developing both grace and strength through its physical side. Many gain from the spiritual side too. However, the ECK teachings give an ECKist other advantages, like the love and guidance of the Mahanta, the Living ECK Master.

The Master's protection reaches into the dream worlds. It touches one's whole life.

The spiritual benefits of ECK outshine those of other paths. The Master's protection reaches into the dream worlds. It touches one's whole life.

So be of a good mind in regard to yoga, because it offers many building blocks for physical and mental development.

Energy Medicine and ECK

What is the difference between energy medicine, as presented in the book by Donna Eden which you have recommended, and other healing modalities that used to be considered as psychic healing—such as chakra and aura balancing, either with crystals or energy, for example?

The boundaries between the various healing arts are becoming progressively less defined, and this causes confusion. What is the central spiritual issue here?

It *is* a fine line.

In a strict sense, all forces of an invisible nature brought to bear upon something or someone to change an outcome are of a psychic nature. The one exception is divine love.

Due to space limitations a detailed argument to show the all-pervasive presence of the psychic arts will not follow.

However, I will give a rule of thumb.

Any conscious or unconscious attempt to change the course or state of a condition—health, political, or spiritual—to gather power to oneself is a negative use of the psychic power.

Service to others in any field, to be a karmaless action, must be done with love and goodwill in the name of the Mahanta.

This is a spiritual art. It depends in the whole upon a pure state of consciousness. Otherwise, there are karmic consequences.

Healers in any line need to learn the practice of detachment. No, that's not to say coldness. True detachment comes from real compassion for others.

In reference to a book like Donna Eden's *Energy Medicine*, I give a *guideline*:

One's risk of incurring karma is not a factor if an individual tries her techniques only upon himself or consenting family members. This small circle may also include close friends.

Any time an exchange of money for services takes place, there is a karmic risk. A professional healer has the training to help patients in the right way. Thus, he incurs little risk. One does not want to load his own balance sheet with the karma of others.

The Living ECK Master does encourage ECK chelas to push the envelope. This world is a lab. It's the place to try experiments of all sorts.

Still, a chela who wants to make spiritual progress will practice karmaless actions.

Yes, the lines between the healing arts are ever

Service to others in any field, to be a karmaless action, depends upon a pure state of consciousness.

more a blur, but perhaps the above guideline will clear up some of the confusion.

Spiritual Lesson in Hair Loss

Over the past couple of years, I have developed a receding hairline. Is there a spiritual lesson to my hair loss? Am I working off karma, or is there an imbalance in my life?

Losing hair can teach us to have respect for what many people take for granted.

Hair loss has dogged me ever since I was your age. It finally dawned on me that I had chosen a family where this was a problem for about half the males. A genetic weakness. But I learned to do something about it.

I learned to cut back on fatty foods. It also worked to use a shampoo that cleaned away sebum from the scalp. And to towel dry my hair gently. Nutrition plays a big role, of course.

But a full head of hair is only a superficial adornment. Many fine people are bald. Baldness is a part of their attraction.

Learn to treat yourself gently.

Solve the baldness problem, and down the road comes the greying problem. Learn to treat yourself gently. It really is more important what's inside you than on your head.

The Healing Properties of Patience and Love

What holds us back from receiving all of the gifts of healing and well-being? What are some qualities that allow us to be all that we are?

Patience and love are two qualities that can bring us life-changing approaches, ways, to find peace and spiritual freedom. Patience and love come hard for some of us. So hardship, we find, is of necessity the best teacher, because it removes us from the driver's seat and ignominiously plops us down along the roadside.

Our view of life (passing us by then) is of a meeker—not the right word—rather, humbler sort. Being strong all the time is great. However, weakness forces us to ask for and accept help. In ECK, much of the stuff that holds one back can work itself out in the dream state.

You Exist Because God Loves You

My grandmother passed away recently. I need a way to not be sad yet always have her with me. I don't want to have to think about her passing away. Can you write back to me about this?

In our home, Mother had a plaque on the wall that simply said, "Time heals all wounds." And it does. It's likely that you can see the same about your feelings now about your grandmother passing away several months ago.

There is no quick, easy answer about how to overcome the pain of separation from a loved one. But, before long, the pain does get less. Often it goes completely away.

Life offers *all* of us an unending chain of joy and sorrow. Know that everything is in its rightful place, that a door opens for every one that is shut. Love who you are, what you do, and those who are dear

Know that everything is in its rightful place, that a door opens for every one that is shut.

to you. Don't ever take your family for granted.

I wish I had some great wisdom to give you. The closest anyone can come is to say, "You exist because God loves you." There is wonder and beauty in that.

What the Master Offers

You have spoken about being a holding tank for our karma, to the point where it makes you physically sick. Also, your wife, Joan, wrote about the unique value of the Master to the chela.

In a culture imbued with the tradition of messianism, it's hard to imagine what may lie beyond the concept of a savior who needs to sacrifice himself to save mankind. What are some of the differences between the role of a savior and the way the Mahanta, the Living ECK Master helps people with their karma?

Faith and belief are based on feelings instead of reason. So it's pointless to argue with someone of another religion about the validity of Eckankar over his beliefs.

This being so, it greatly simplifies the matter for us. We do not wish to convince anyone about anything.

It'd largely be a waste of precious time.

The Mahanta, the Living ECK Master offers the chance for spiritual liberation in this lifetime.

To begin with, a fundamental premise in ECK is that reincarnation is a fact. A main tenet of this Christian society is the principle of one life, one time. These two positions are miles apart. They can never be in agreement.

So what does the Mahanta, the Living ECK Master offer an ECK chela (spiritual student)?

It's first and foremost the chance for spiritual liberation. And what's more, it's possible in this very same lifetime. That is a significant benefit. By the time a seeker comes across the ECK teachings, he has reached a state of consciousness that realizes the real need for self-responsibility. It is within the order of Soul's evolution.

For example, what loving parent would knowingly punish one child for the misdeeds of another? Each child is responsible for his own deeds.

The main benefit the Master then offers is freedom from the wheel of karma and reincarnation. That is salvation in Eckankar.

Each is responsible for his own deeds.

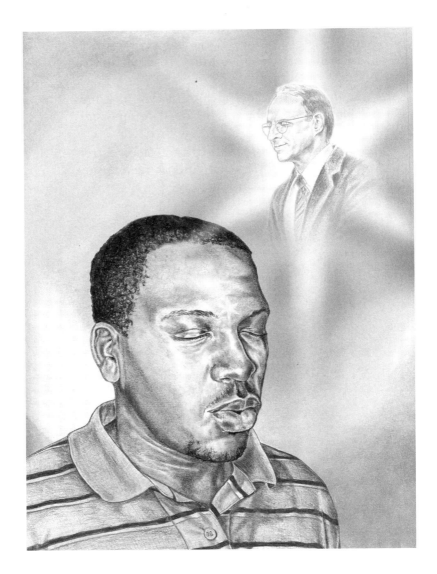

Whenever you feel under psychic attack, you can protect yourself. Sing HU, the love song to God, in silence, and fix your inner attention upon the Mahanta.

6

SPIRITUAL
PROTECTION

*J*ust what is an evil spirit? Do those who play
with the psychic forces have protection? And how do
you view the craze about the Harry Potter books and
films and their simplistic portrayal of the power of
the psychic arts?

An evil spirit is a destructive entity without a
current physical body. Think of a robber, a thief, or
a monster. It wants to exercise power over the weak
or gullible, to play a devilish trick or take command
of a human body for its own devious ends.

Like here, in all the lower worlds there are small-
time and big-time crooks. A sensible person avoids
both.

Those who play with the psychic forces are on
their own, to gather such knowledge that proves to
them they do not want to go there again. That's the
way of learning on earth. The Mahanta, the Living
ECK Master warns about psychic dangers, yet he
lets individuals pursue their interests. He gives
freedom to all.

*The
Mahanta
warns about
psychic
dangers, yet
he gives
freedom
to all.*

At some point, the psychic dabbler comes to his senses and calls upon the Master for help. Then the Master will examine the situation, to see what is the best, most instructive way to lead the disillusioned one to safety.

The Harry Potter books and films present the two sides of the psychic powers: the good and evil. For all that, it's still a study, albeit superficial, of the psychic forces.

The Harry Potter books and films present the two sides of the psychic powers: the good and evil.

There is an upside to the Harry Potter books: they create a strong desire in children to learn to read. Impatient for the movie, they devour the latest book. The craze will run its cycle, of course. When the dust settles, there'll be a whole new generation of readers, who will move on to other areas of interest and so enrich their lives.

Children will clamor to see the Harry Potter films. Explain the pitfalls and outright dangers of the psychic arts before they watch them. Key words: "before they watch them."

Protection from Attacks

In my family the elder ones believe in supernatural things. For many years they made it clear to everyone in the family that some members practiced witchcraft and had been controlling the family since its beginning. This planted deep seeds of fear in our consciousness. To make matters worse, the self-righteous ones accuse many members of the family of witchcraft.

First of all, is there such a person as a witch, and does evil attack us in our family? Also, did it affect me and my immediate brothers and sisters? And what can I do to help solve the problems of my family?

Unfortunately, there is such a person as a witch. In fact, a witch is anyone who tries to control another by overt or hidden means.

Witchcraft is in every country. It is a practice employed by "good" members of a religious community who use force or guile to make others accept their beliefs. Needless to say, it is a spiritual violation.

What gives a witch power? Fear.

A culture that is saturated in a fear of supernatural things produces a people open to the power of witchcraft.

Beyond such a susceptibility, however, there is an inherent psychic power in witchcraft. It can have effects, or force, within the domain of the witch, be it a witch in the family, one next door, or in the neighborhood.

A simple answer, of course, is to leave such surroundings.

However, such an answer is simplistic. That is especially so when a victim has a duty to others in the family and must bear that responsibility. A witch trying to cast spells upon a chela (spiritual student) of the Mahanta, the Living ECK Master will, in time, come to grief.

The power of witchcraft will gradually die out in a strong community of ECK initiates.

Love for the Mahanta is the antidote for fear. This sweet love grows strong through the daily practice of the Spiritual Exercises of ECK.

Whenever you feel yourself under psychic attack by a witch, you can protect yourself. Sing HU, the love song to God, in silence, and fix your whole inner attention upon the loving radiance of the Mahanta. I am always with you.

A witch is anyone who tries to control another by overt or hidden means. It is a spiritual violation.

HU, a Powerful Defense

Can you explain briefly what the word HU means and its use as protection?

HU, a sacred name for God, is popular among members of ECKANKAR, especially in Africa. Black magic is a very powerful force there, able to wreak havoc. An ECKist who is the object of a curse can sing this word *HU* and also picture a shield of white light between himself and the black magician. Or he can simply sing HU and put his inner attention upon the Mahanta.

The white light is the Light of God. HU is the Sound of God. The Light and Sound are the two most trusted pillars of protection that one can ever find.

People sing HU quietly or aloud to receive protection from trouble or danger on the street, at work, or in the home.

People in Europe, Australia, and the Americas also sing HU quietly or aloud to receive protection from trouble or danger on the street, at work, or in the home.

HU is a powerful defense.

Sensitivity

I have a lot of trouble in my room. I am fourteen years old and still have nightmares and see things, such as a ghost. I do a visualization technique in which I put the ECK Masters around the windows and doors, but it doesn't always work. I still get afraid. What can I do?

You're at an age of high sensitivity. It can take the form of nightmares or seeing ghosts, a problem that my sister and I also ran into from about the age of twelve to fifteen.

A small night-light or two for your bedroom is a way to keep the powers of night at bay. Another is to have a pet in your room overnight. And keep up the spiritual exercises.

Don't watch horror shows on TV at all, but try to watch upbeat programs of comedy, nature, or sports. Many soft drinks are high in caffeine, which makes for tense nerves—so replace harmful soft drinks with herbal teas or fruit drinks. Take multivitamins and multiminerals. Be sure to get enough rest and exercise.

The above suggestions can bring you more calm. Put extra attention on peace and quiet for another year or two, after which your sensitivity will balance out.

White Magic and Black Magic

You've said that when someone is trying to direct the ECK, it is a form of white magic. Elsewhere you've defined it as black magic. What is the difference between the two? How does this relate to giving love with strings attached?

Is it OK, as a spiritual exercise, to visualize the best-case scenario of a situation? At what point can a self-created spiritual exercise turn to white or black magic?

Carefully consider the context of such answers. First of all, an ECK initiate should move into a position of karmaless action. That means doing everything in the name of the Master.

It is the easy way.

White magic is with an intent to do some good. But note that it is not done in the Master's name

> White magic is with an intent to do some good. When attitude drifts into having power and control over others, the deed slips into black magic.

at all. When one's attitude drifts into thoughts of having power and control over others, the deed then slips into black magic.

Still, there is no sharp line of demarcation between black and white karma. There is also plenty of gray area. That is because everything is in constant flux, changing in some measure, either a little or a lot.

Black magic, at its darkest, seeks to harm or control others right at the onset.

Giving a gift or doing a "kindness" is in the grayish white area of white magic. Please understand that there are degrees of good deeds and white karma, and so also are there degrees of retribution for practicing them. So do all your giving in the Master's name.

Yes, it is OK to expect the best outcome for a situation. But also remember to respond positively to whatever the result.

Value of Discrimination

People have told me about severe problems with psychic attacks from "astral witches" and also from other people. Are these psychic irritations or excuses for problems in life? Or are these real attacks by real people? What should I tell these people?

You cannot save people from themselves.

It's tempting to want to do more to help people in need. The truth, however, is that you cannot save them from themselves.

Fear makes us susceptible to invasion by unwelcome forces, such as the psychic attacks described by some people. Fear has many faces. It may be a fear of not being loved. To compensate, the individual will toss aside all discrimination as to the choice of friends in the outer life. This lack of discrimination also carries over to the inner life. Doors there open, then, to psychic attacks.

Another fear may be fear of loss. So the individual clamps on to material goods and relationships long past their natural cycle. To explain, it means to hang on to something after it has become harmful or painful beyond limits.

These two examples show attachment. It is one of the five passions of the mind.

So what do you do?

Encouraging the person to sing HU, the love song to God, will strengthen the force of love in him. Love, in time, dispels fear. Healing will follow.

The psychic attacks are real, but the entities may or may not be the imagined "other people." On the Astral level, the power of imagination is stronger than here. So an entity can easily mock up the appearance of someone the individual hates, fears, or doesn't want to lose.

It's a face-saving measure. Now the person has an excuse to refuse responsibility for his own poor choices, passions, or indecision.

Again, what do you do?

Understand that all healing comes from the ECK, which works in Its own time, place, and way. Nothing will, or can, be done unless changes first occur within the individual's own state of consciousness.

You can suggest the person seek help from a professional counselor if there is a serious imbalance or see a doctor to check out possible health problems. Speak and act with love, but do not get caught up in the other's physical, emotional, or mental problems.

Nothing will, or can, be done unless changes first occur within the individual's own state of consciousness.

Keeping Your Liberty

My brothers and I got a Ouija board, and I was just wondering, are Ouija boards safe? Some people say it attracts evil spirits and other bad things.

A Ouija board is a dangerous "toy."

Yes, it does attract evil spirits (destructive entities without current physical bodies), who, at best, play harmless tricks on people. At worst, they attack the Soul whose body it is, drive out that Soul, then take over the body. If the owner Soul is too strong to drive out completely, the evil spirits will try to settle for a chunk of body and mind space.

Possession by evil spirits accounts for people's sudden change in personality.

Then there's the split personality. That's when one or more evil spirits and the owner Soul take turns in the driver's seat, like driving a car. Such a person is no fun to be around. In fact, many like that land in mental asylums.

Another evil spirit may drive one to do a crime. Then, when the owner Soul of that human body sits in prison, the entity may leave to look for more action, for another sucker playing with a Ouija board.

Ouija boards, séances, and automatic handwriting are all like loaded guns in the hands of children.

It's all fun and games for an evil spirit.

Ouija boards, séances, and automatic handwriting are all like loaded guns in the hands of children.

From a spiritual point of view, no highly developed spiritual being would allow another entity to take away his liberty. But that's just what a Ouija board sets the stage to do. What advanced individual would risk the loss of freedom?

Do yourself a favor: put the Ouija board in the trash. It's a deadly "toy," the same as school-yard drugs. Don't be a sucker of the negative power.

Everything Is a Gift from God

Sometimes when I am playing alone, I look up and see someone I don't know. It isn't always the same person, but there are some I see more often than others. I can make them go away if I close my eyes. Then when I open them again, they're gone.

I also sense if something bad is going to happen the next day, usually to someone I don't know. I don't know their names or exactly what will happen, but I know if they are a boy, girl, man, or woman. Then I hear something on the news about it. I also feel like someone is watching me from behind my back all the time. Are these things real or just my imagination? They make me feel afraid a lot of the time.

My mom tells me to sing HU, but even when I do, it feels like someone is right beside my face, and I get scared and stop singing HU. What is happening to me, and how can I feel less afraid?

Are the things I see a gift from God, or are they illusions—my mind playing tricks on me?

Everything is a gift from God. Please understand that even the Kal Niranjan is a servant of God and must answer to the ECK, the Voice of God. The Kal helps us face our weaknesses so that we may grow in strength.

Another thing to understand is illusion. The things of this world are real, but seen in a wrong light. People think that they're one thing when, in fact, there's more to them than meets the eye. It'd take pages to make the idea of illusion clearer to you. But let's just say they are real.

Now the challenge is to understand what is happening to you.

The things of this world are real, but seen in a wrong light. There's more to them than meets the eye.

Young people are sometimes troubled by nightmares or other strange things. Their minds are still an open window to some past life.

Young people your age are sometimes troubled by nightmares or other strange things. Their minds are still an open window to some past life when they trained as a priest or priestess to develop their powers of prophecy.

This ability was the "second sight." It requires a strong person who won't be swept here and there by his emotions. But what to do?

Ask your parents to double-check your nutrition. Stop taking foods that stress the nerves like chocolate or soft drinks (often loaded with caffeine). Also cut down on the amount of other candies, and try fruit instead. Here, I may also suggest organic fruit, because regular fruit often has herbicides and pesticides on it.

Look also to the shows you watch on TV. Those with violence disturb the natural harmony of the emotional body.

Nor are computers the absolute boon to society that some claim, because the electricity sends out jagged waves that interrupt the normal nerve networks of sensitive people.

And be sure to get enough sleep.

It's about Love

I have been taking steps off the written path and onto my own inner path. I am beginning to understand things my own way.

Eckankar is the only religion I know of that gives people the particular tools and techniques that it does. For me Soul Travel was an important step toward believing in spiritual freedom. Understanding past lives keeps us from feeling powerless. Looking for waking dreams in everyday life gives us reassurance that we are not alone. And I have learned from Eckankar about karma and its effects on people.

Although it is important to recognize that past ties exist, is it more essential to focus on allowing love into a karmic situation? Am I right in thinking the only thing I need to focus on is love and how to work with it?

You're so right—the path of ECK is about love. God's love.

It's true that the outer teachings are an important mainstay in a chela's spiritual life, because they lead to the essential inner ones. The outer ECK teachings give vital info to a truth seeker about karma, Soul Travel, dreams, the ECK-Vidya. These are the rungs of the spiritual ladder. The rungs, and the ladder as a whole, lead upward. Upward, to love. Yet the rungs remain an important part of the ladder. They will see future use.

And why?

Because the stresses of life knock right back to the ground many a one who's discovered love. Believe it or not, the chela slips out of his once-exalted state of divine love.

Here's one of those cosmic chuckles: it's when a chela's ego gets onstage. Typically, he'll say something like this: "I'm a Master in my own right." He'll then also try to separate the Living ECK Master from the Mahanta. The Master is one. He's hardly a schizophrenic like this chela, for that's what this sort of chela is: a spiritual schizophrenic.

In time, the chela finds that what he so proudly called his own inner path wasn't that at all. At least, it's not at all what he'd expected it to be.

So he's taken a lot of time and trouble to go on

The path of ECK is about God's love. The outer teachings are an important mainstay because they lead to the essential inner ones.

another detour. But the Master's not concerned. He's seen it a hundred times before.

Love is the goal in ECK, and only a few chelas have found this love in spite of all their imaginings to the contrary.

Someone who wishes the ECK to guide him along the path of eternal truth must become like a child. It takes no thought for the morrow. Today is all there is. Would a young child set conditions upon his parent about love? I don't think so. Tomorrow will be what tomorrow will be, so it's never given a second thought.

The way of love both gives to and receives from the very highest source of it available anywhere.

The Mahanta, the Living ECK Master will often keep the screen pulled down so the chela (spiritual student) doesn't learn of some "evil" to befall him tomorrow. If the lesson is necessary, it's necessary. The Master won't show (reveal) the imminent appearance of karma because why add the fear of dread to the chela's load? There is kindness and consideration in all the Master does.

It's an expression of love. It's in return for the chela's unwavering, unconditional love for the Mahanta, the Living ECK Master.

Such is the way of love. It both gives to and receives from the very highest source of it available anywhere—Sugmad (God).

Enjoy yourself, but also understand that the responsibility to help or harm yourself, either physically or spiritually, rests mainly in your hands.

7

PAST LIVES AND KARMIC LESSONS

People reincarnate to resolve karma created in past lifetimes. But, observing world events, it seems people are creating more karma for themselves. Will people learn to work together while resolving their karma? If we take responsibility for our actions, then when will our karma be finished so reincarnation is no longer necessary?

The whole process of refining Souls through resolving karma made in past lives is a slow, careful one. The mills of karma grind slowly, but exceedingly fine.

Yes, people are very busy every day creating new karma for themselves. The reason is they overreact to every slight. They show a lack of respect first for themselves, then for others. They need still to develop the quality of grace. Grace and respect are two signs of a mature spiritual individual, whatever his religion or beliefs.

Karma works itself off by levels, through the

Karma works itself off by levels, through the hard experiences of life—the University of Hard Knocks.

hard experiences of life—the University of Hard Knocks. A Soul that completes a certain level of purification then graduates to a higher level of choice, experience, and service.

You'll find that many leaders in politics belong to the school of adolescent Souls. It explains their shortsighted and irresponsible behavior as the supposed representatives of their electorate. But they too will someday move above their own limitations.

Illness as Karma

I think the ECK, Divine Spirit, knew I was going to do something wrong before I did it. So I got sick to pay for my future karma. Can this happen?

Yes, it can. If you know that thoughts are real, it should make you think twice before even thinking of doing wrong.

Most of our illnesses are from something we've done in the past.

Most of our illnesses, though, are from something we've done in the past—such as eating too much of a certain food that our particular body cannot digest. At your age, I ate as much candy, cake, or pie as possible, because I never truly believed they would hurt me. They did.

You'll do better all around if you take it a little easy in everything. Enjoy yourself, but also understand that the responsibility to help or harm yourself, either physically or spiritually, rests mainly in your hands.

So first ask the Mahanta inwardly about the right way to act. Your life can then become easier and far richer in more ways than you could ever imagine.

Responsibility for
Ourselves in Daily Life

What is the limit of responsibility in our daily life? I'm referring to our responsibility for the results of our own actions. For example, if we purchase a product that has been produced by a company that treats its workforce unfairly or restricts their freedom, to what level are we responsible for this by supporting such a company? This also includes poor treatment of animals and unnecessary damage to the environment.

Psychic waves always wash over the earth. A common feature of people out to save the earth is their duplicity.

For example, there are accounts of environmentalist tours to a lovely place that ended with trash littering the landscape. Those are dishonest people.

Another example is people who rail against auto pollution but own and drive SUVs or large, expensive cars. Or also, environmental advocates who preach the development of the inner cities, while they live out in the country on large, sweeping estates. They are dishonest people.

They don't walk the talk.

Of course, such people often command a large group of followers who are the willing voices, hands, and feet of carrying forth the environmental message.

Look also at the proponents of electric cars. No pollution! Sounds good, doesn't it? But how to charge a car's batteries? With power created by fossil fuels or nuclear generators, since solar and wind power can supply but a fraction of our society's need for electricity to power lights, TVs, air conditioning, computers, etc.

Dishonest people don't walk the talk.

Cars cause pollution? Horses in cities once resulted in city blocks reserved for manure piles stacked high. Flies.

Global warming? The largest contributors seldom spoken of are solar bursts and volcanic eruptions under the seas. Scientists are only now discovering the frequency with which the latter occur.

On the other hand, a clean planet is like a clean body. It's a noble cause to help get and keep it clean, but be careful of emotional entanglements from the psychic, emotional, waves that also pollute the earth.

Seeing Past Lives

I would like to see my past lives. How do I go about this?

No matter what we were in the past during any other life, we are spiritually greater today.

When we practice the Spiritual Exercises of ECK faithfully, the Inner Master will open us up to those things that are important to see concerning past lives. Most of them need not concern us. No matter what we were in the past during any other life, we are spiritually greater today.

The wealth and position we enjoyed in past lives mean nothing unless we know how to lift ourselves from materialism into the higher worlds. This does not mean to shun the good things of this life—family, home, wealth. God loves the rich man as much as the poor. We get no special benefits if we fall for the negative tricks of asceticism or unusual austerities.

We live the spiritual life beginning where we are today. We look to see the hand of Divine Spirit, the ECK, guiding us toward the greater consciousness, which leads us to becoming a more direct vehicle for Spirit.

Actions Aligned with ECK

I have heard the saying "eye for eye, tooth for tooth." What techniques can be used so our actions are aligned with the ECK? How can we forgive ourselves and not feel guilty when we judge or hurt someone we love?

"Eye for eye, tooth for tooth" is the strict Law of Karma. This law is to teach people self-responsibility. It's unforgiving. Under it, people hope others get punished.

The strict Law of Karma is to teach people self-responsibility.

A higher law is the Law of Love. With this law comes the understanding that indeed what will be will be. But the difference here is that we do not wish or expect others to get punished for their misdeeds. Instead, we give them love in return.

How does this work out in daily life?

If someone cheats us out of our property or goods, we will, of course, try to get it back by whatever legal means possible. The difference is that we will do so without feelings of hatred or anger. Such feelings tie us to the strict Law of Karma.

How can you forgive yourself? Just do it. Apologize, then, for your thoughtless behavior and try to do better next time. Don't just try—do it.

And always apologize with thoughts of the Master's love for you.

Suffering and Karma

My daughter saw an animal shelter in our city in which the dogs suffer from very bad care. Since we both love animals, my daughter wants to know why these dogs have to suffer so badly and live under such cruel conditions.

When people suffer and live in bad circumstances, I can explain it with the Law of Karma and rebirth. But how can those animals have broken the spiritual laws? Could you please explain if animals create karma too?

A Soul may intentionally choose a hard life to learn more about love, wisdom, and charity.

Suffering is not always a direct result of breaking a spiritual law. Even though everyone gets *adi karma*, the primal karma that starts us off in our first lifetime, there is far more to the spiritual journey. A Soul may intentionally choose a hard life to learn more about love, wisdom, and charity. Pain, like joy, is simply a tool in the toolbox of karma and rebirth.

To grow spiritually, we move beyond a strict acceptance of karma and thus take the high road to God.

You can, as spiritual beings, try to make your city shelter a more livable place. Talk to the owner or manager. If that goes nowhere, visit or call your city hall. Each time, ask the Mahanta what steps to take, then go one step at a time until the conditions in the city's animal shelter are more humane.

An ECKist need not be a helpless cog in the machinery of life. You answer to a higher law: divine love. Use your spiritual powers of creation for the good of all.

Learning to Pay Attention

I had a camera stolen from me in Europe, and I was wondering why this sort of thing happens. Is it just because I'm not paying attention, or is there some deeper karma involved?

The karma here was simply about learning to pay attention. If something is valuable to you—a camera, a loved one, a state of mind—it pays not to neglect it.

In the future, no doubt, you'll pay special attention to any new camera because you still feel the pain of loss from your old one. The loss of a camera is a cheap lesson if it gets across the lesson of being careful with those things that have a special value for us.

Precious is as precious does.

Protecting Yourself

What effect does playing video and computer games or watching TV and movies have on us? Is there any karma involved? Are there ways to protect oneself yet still play or watch them?

All activity involves karma—good or bad.

That said, there seems no way to escape it. But, yes, there is. That is, to do everything in the name of the Mahanta.

Easy?

Actually, no. A problem arises when one gets so caught up in the passion of doing something that it begins to take over his life. He'll always come up with a good reason why a passion out of control is a necessary activity. In short, he's kidding himself.

That's the nature of illusion. It clouds people's minds.

In the heyday of comic books, in the 1940s and 1950s, alarmists railed against them for ruining the young. Those youth are sixty and seventy today. The only thing that seems to ruin them is hard living and old age.

Before comics the day's evil was dime novels.

Then came radio adventure serials.

All activity involves karma—good or bad. There seems no way to escape it. But, yes, there is.

Next, TV.

Now, computer and video games.

So the more things change, the more they stay the same.

What, then, does one do?

What, then, does one do? Walk the middle path, being aware not to stray from it too far to the left or right. Observe, how much of your time does computing require? Is there time to keep up with (noncomputer) friends, get out among people, keep fit with exercise?

Computers like to take over. Don't let them. There's too much to do and learn outside of a computer's case.

Can We Cancel Out Karma?

When you think a bad thought or say something negative, then realize the karma you've created for yourself, can you cancel it out by saying Baraka Bashad (May the blessings be)? Or is there something else you can do to correct it?

Yes, if the root of the impurity that caused the negative thought is gone.

That is a big if.

I do not wish to leave the impression that one can kiss and make it better by simply mouthing Baraka Bashad or May the blessings be. It is not that easy. Let me explain.

A negative thought or word or deed expressed reveals a blemish in some part of one's consciousness. Such things stick like bad habits. They are quite comfortable where they are, thank you, and have no intention of getting booted out so easily.

Has a certain tune ever gone around and around

in your head until you thought it would drive you crazy? A Baraka Bashad would likely not disperse it just like that.

No, it is a matter of sustained attention. What is the best way to do that, do you suppose?

Yes, by putting your whole attention upon the Mahanta until the negative thought gives up its hold on you. Depending upon how deeply it is lodged inside you, you may continue with this mental fast for either a short or a long time.

Kinds of Karma that Affect You

Do we hold our country's karma as well as our own? Do I accrue karma when my government takes an action, because I'm a member of that community? How does this affect me as an ECKist?

You most certainly do hold your country's karma as well as your own. On top of that, there is other karma too.

Family karma comes to mind right away. But any political, religious, social, racial, ethnic, geographic, professional, trade, or other grouping lends its own weight to your karmic load.

In fact, all kinds of karma affect you.

The enormity of it would be crushing if we dwelled upon it. But there's no need to. The karma is part of the divine plan to strengthen Soul spiritually.

Karma is part of the divine plan to strengthen Soul spiritually.

Yes, it may be the lot of people to accrue karma when their government takes an action. In time of war, for example, some may be called into the military to serve their country.

How, then, is it possible for an ECKist to keep from making karma?

Easy. Doing everything in the name of the Mahanta will guide you past every pitfall. I do hope this helps you to understand.

Reincarnation and Gender

With each physical reincarnation, do the higher bodies (e.g., astral, causal, mental) die, change, or transform? Can these bodies change appearance at will? Also, in what form does gender exist in the higher worlds, and at what point does gender end?

In general, the higher the world, the longer the duration of all within it.

So with each physical reincarnation, the higher bodies usually remain intact. And yes, they can change appearance at will. There's more to this than your question implies, but trying to understand it with a human mind would be mind-bending, to say the very least.

Gender is all-important on the Astral Plane, the area of emotions and passionate feelings. But it becomes increasingly less important on the higher planes.

And when does gender end?

It ends when Soul reaches the Soul Plane, first of the spiritual worlds. There, each Soul is whole. The lower worlds of distinctions and differences have vanished.

Your questions show a deep interest in the miracle of the ECK's, Holy Spirit's, creation. The Mahanta, the Inner Master, will reveal more to you about the makeup of creation when you are spiritually ready to receive it.

When does gender end? When Soul reaches the Soul Plane. There, each Soul is whole.

Facing Our Fears

How do I overcome my fear of swimming or water with the help of the Mahanta? I have gone for swimming lessons in Singapore but dropped out because of my fear. Now in New Zealand, I have decided to take swimming lessons again and will try not to drop out.

Our fears may look foolish to others; theirs, in turn, may appear foolish to us. So where do they come from? And much more important, what can you do about them?

Most fears have their origin in a past life. For example, a fear of fire may signal a long-ago death by fire. A dislike of neckties, hanging. A dread of deep water, death by drowning. Such fears are real. Strong ones are a big stumbling block, while others may only have a small impact upon us and are merely a nuisance.

Most fears have their origin in a past life.

All people must face their own fears at some time, sooner or later. The ECK Masters know that, so they seldom interfere in such matters, because it would rob a chela of an important lesson needed to unfold spiritually.

Even so, the Mahanta *is* standing by if he sees you are sincere about overcoming your problem.

What kind of help does he offer?

It can be of many kinds, such as encouragement or providing a dream experience that saves wear and tear on your physical body. You may expect to receive tips and advice too. So stay alert.

At bedtime, open your heart to love. It is your passkey to the Master. Then go to sleep peacefully.

Karma and Our Inner Bodies

Soul exists because God loves It. Soul has the Physical, Astral, Causal, Mental, and Etheric bodies. How does this affect the karmic load, especially in reincarnation? When the physical body dies, how does this affect the other bodies?

The individual Soul, you know, has a body on each of the planes you mentioned, because a body can only exist in a world, or plane, of like substance.

Now think of karma, whatever chunk of it happens to be on one plane or another, as a schoolbag full of books. Each chunk of karma, like one book, is like one part of a whole body of other karma (books).

This karma, as a collective whole, is all the lessons that Soul (a person) needs in order to become a more godlike being.

So when the physical body dies, any karma (like a book) not completely learned is put in the schoolbag and carried home (in this case, to the Astral Plane). There's homework between lives. It's a chance to review the day's (or past physical life's) lessons, take them to heart, and try to do better in (earth's) school tomorrow (the next lifetime in the Physical Plane—perhaps on earth again).

At death the main karma, by which an individual was learning the purity of spirit in an earlier life, moves to the plane above. At rebirth, all unlearned lessons of that karma continue.

As an ECKist you know there's a shortcut to this tiresome cycle of karma and reincarnation. The Mahanta, the Living ECK Master can show those with the eyes to see and the ears to hear a better way.

Much of one's karma in daily life can thus work off in the dream state. It's less wear and tear on the body.

There's homework between lives. It's a chance to review the past life's lessons, take them to heart, and try to do better next lifetime.

Gift and Lesson from Atlantis

Ever since I can remember, I've been able to see colors emanating from everything. Often it's the color amethyst. Why do I see all these colors other people can't? What do they mean, and how can I use this sight so it may benefit me?

Thank you for your letter about the colors you see. It's an ability you developed during several lives in Atlantis, where crystals were the power that propelled those times, much as electricity and nuclear power are a mainstay today. Seeing the ECK Current as big and little explosions of color was a common ability among all in Atlantis.

The spiritual lesson in Atlantis was for those who specialized in harnessing the power of crystals—scientists, priests, and engineers—to learn how to use it for the good of *others*.

It's the same challenge today for those who bring a special gift into this lifetime.

The color amethyst has a natural affinity for the Etheric Plane. That's the fountain where intuition originates. The lesson is how to use that potential to help others and not control them in any way.

That is the lesson for all people, for all have gifts and talents unique to them. But it's in the manner of their use that determines whether they, the users, wish to go the way of love or power.

The ECK will help you deal with your gift, if you so wish.

The lesson is how to use that potential to help others and not control them in any way.

Keeping Your Face toward God

Can we actually rid ourselves of all our past-life karma in one lifetime and not have to reincarnate again?

*Many people
of the frozen-
food society
wonder,* Why
didn't this
work for me?

Yes, if the person keeps his face toward the Light of God and listens to the Sound. Many people who go on the path of God are basically of the frozen-food society. They want to do it for about five to ten minutes or five to ten days. Then they lose interest. They wonder, *Why didn't this work for me?*

They give their life over to something that is going to change them forever, and if in five to ten days nothing happens, they get so disillusioned they give up the path to God. Then they say that it doesn't work.

That's sometimes the nature of the person who hasn't lived in the lower worlds very long and hasn't many past lives to his or her credit.

It's difficult in my role as spiritual leader. There are just a few people who can really recognize the gift of the Inner and Outer Master. Those who can, accept it. Those who can't, reject it.

The people who reject it are usually those who criticize and make fun of the spiritual leader because they don't know better. But the spiritual leader never holds it against them. He was that way too once. It's just part of the human condition.

Is Karma Ever Finished?

Is there a way to know when our negative karma from past lives is finished in the lower worlds? As an ECKist, I would like to serve the ECK (Divine Spirit) as purely as possible, but if the heart is clouded with impurities due to past karma, how would one know when one is acting purely?

The underlying question you ask is this: Does a High Initiate in ECK still have karma? The direct answer is yes.

Next, the question arises: Well, what's the initiation about if not to free Soul from the bonds of karma? The simple answer is that the individual has gained the opportunity to work out the remaining karma in this lifetime and never have to return to the material worlds unless for a spiritual service to Sugmad (God).

It explains why the behavior of some initiates is of such a questionable grade. Also, why some leave the path of ECK.

No one, even in Eckankar, has a place confirmed in heaven by merit of an outer ECK initiation. What a High Initiate can enjoy, though, is heavenly. That means the pure Light and musical Sound of the ECK Current in the first of the true heavenly worlds.

The Spiritual Exercises of ECK are the key to spiritual liberation. They are the means for Soul to meet the Mahanta in these pure worlds, for the Mahanta is your lifeline to the purifying power and love of the Sound Current. Only the Mahanta, the Living ECK Master can take anyone to Sugmad.

Some will dispute this truth and try to go it on their own. They are also the ones who leave ECK.

What can be more important to a spiritual being than the Spiritual Exercises of ECK? They help clean up the house of five bodies inside you, to prepare you to meet the Mahanta in the Holy Sanctuary.

That sanctuary is not any temple or church of wood or stone. It's your heart.

So walk with love and confidence throughout life. I am always with you.

What's the initiation about? The individual has gained the opportunity to work out the remaining karma in this lifetime.

A relationship is like a garden in that both need constant attention. Both see days of sunshine and rain.

8
FAMILY AND
RELATIONSHIPS

Why is love so hard on some people? I love my family and friends, but sometimes I forget myself. How can you tell if you are wanted?

You already hint at the answer in the third part of your question. This issue bothers a lot of people. Replace "wanted" with "loved." It is very revealing.

Love is hard because we make it so. The uncertainty about being loved shapes the way we act toward others. Some of us are rebellious to the things that our families hold dear. Others of us go to another extreme. We love and nurture others to the neglect of our own well-being. Time often gets us back on track, though.

So what can you do to get back on track as soon as possible and be happy?

One cannot buy love through caring for and nurturing others. Those two qualities can be of the real kind if they come from someone who is a magnet for love.

Uncertainty about being loved shapes the way we act toward others.

Look at others as if they are carriers of the Mahanta's love to you. In fact, they are. The next point is important. You must consciously open your heart to the Master's love, which is always and forever flowing out to you like a quiet mountain stream.

It's easy to do.

Let's make a spiritual exercise for yourself. In your mind and heart, watch this quiet stream of the Master's love flow gently into your heart and being. It will change you.

Learning from Others

Why is it that some people are close to us and some are not?

You're seeing associations from past lives come into play.

Yet life's best teachers are the people who toss thorns in our path. So long as it makes us sore, there's a spiritual lesson that pleads for an airing.

The people around you are in your company for give-and-take. Let's say you shrink from the presence of a certain individual. Look at it from the other side. For good or ill, your mutual dealings are bringing changes to both parties, even if ever so slight.

Look behind the screen. What is really going on?

Furthermore, once the karma between you is satisfied, your association will wither on the vine, like a cucumber without water. Karma is just that exacting.

Karma's deck of cards deals both hearts and clubs, friends as well as enemies.

Your dear ones are old friends. You've been to-

Karma's deck of cards deals both hearts and clubs, friends as well as enemies.

gether before. You've tasted the good times and bad, the victories and defeats, the joys and heartaches. Together you gained in spiritual ways. At other times, though, you managed to trip over each other's feet, crying aloud in pain. Then you drew apart. But your hearts did mend. Your friendship was the stronger for it.

Enemies and friends act like spiritual coaches. They round out the rough spots in Soul's unfoldment.

The Mahanta teaches through others. So pay careful attention to when sparks fly, because some important thing in you—perhaps courage or forgiveness—needs some polish.

Enemies and friends act like spiritual coaches. They round out the rough spots in Soul's unfoldment.

Insights on Patience and Love

Can you give a spiritual insight on: How to expand into a more patient, more loving being? How to let go of attitudes or people that are hurting me spiritually? How to let go of them without having feelings of sin or guilt?

Yours is an excellent question. It bothers others too. The key is "without having feelings of sin and guilt," because that phrase puts the concern into down-to-earth living.

Notice how changes in nature are most often over eons of time. The heat and cold of desert mountains set rocks to tumble—one here, another there. Eons pass. But the ages see those mountains turn into gentle, rolling hills.

Less often does nature change earth's landscape by explosion or upheaval. Such rapid change leaves scars upon the land that resist healing.

When possible, let those people go without slamming the door. The exception, of course, is in cases where those people's attitudes are a serious threat to your spiritual well-being. That may require a firm "no more of that—good-bye."

Otherwise, the less harmful associations can be let to dry up and wither away.

Be unavailable to such people. Ignore their messages and invitations. Don't give ear to their rumblings or complaints. Maybe they'll get the hint.

With those who linger, be firm but kind.

Facing Ourselves

What should I do when people pick on me physically, emotionally, mentally, and verbally? This problem seems to have a strong hold on my life.

Life, through other people and situations, faces us with ourselves.

Life, through other people and situations, faces us with ourselves.

It makes the weak stronger. The shy learn to be more outgoing. Helpless people are thrown upon their own resources, forcing them to help themselves. A popular song some years ago said, "Freedom's just another word for nothing left to lose." It was talking about an inner frame of mind.

Be strong to the strong. Show kindness to the weak. Use resourcefulness to deal with people and situations that cause you problems. Life brings us face-to-face with ourselves.

In your case, keep your attention firmly fixed upon the Mahanta. Sing HU, a love song to God, inwardly at the first sign of trouble. (HU is pronounced like the word *hue* and sung in a long, drawn-out note.)

You need to gain the wisdom to learn when to show strength, give a helping hand, or use your head to steer clear of danger. Once we've cast our lot to go a certain direction in life, it takes a steady determination to turn back a negative momentum and live for a good purpose in the future.

If it's any consolation, every Soul must eventually face every test. The only salvation lies in keeping HU upon our lips.

Remember, the Master is always with you. Even in your darkest hour.

Life Partners

How important is it to date or marry someone in the same religion as me?

This life is for the gaining of spiritual experience.

Life partners often—nearly always—reach an agreement with others important to their mutual spiritual unfoldment long before either of them becomes aware of it on earth. But destiny is not fixed. Each has to find the other, often sorting through many possible choices.

Destiny is not fixed.

An ECKist will, of course, consider both ECKists and non-ECKists as a life partner. Most Souls agree to total amnesia before their return to earth in new bodies. The reason for that is to avoid old biases and hatreds. Amnesia gives one a fresh start.

Your spirituality depends upon yourself. Someone in your religion may or may not be the right choice for you at a given time, so look around. Ask the Mahanta, the Inner Master, to help you weigh the spiritual advantages of each potential life partner.

Family Karma

How can people find out whether they love truly or not, and why are they hasty to get married? Why do I find myself in my family instead of another family? And what can a child do to keep from suffering so much when their parents divorce?

Love is blind and probably always will be. The only way to find out anything in life is to go ahead and get the experience. Nothing is ever lost. Each experience can teach us valuable lessons about ourselves, painful though they may be.

Impatience and blindness (a lack of experience in such matters) are the reason for hasty marriages. There's little that can be done about it.

Why are you in your family and not another?

Why are you in your family and not another? It's for the simple reason that you and your parents agreed to it before this lifetime ever began. Somehow, all of you saw a spiritual reason for being together. So in contemplation ask the Mahanta to show you in some way what some of those reasons were. It will make you a person of more love, wisdom, and compassion.

How to keep from suffering so much when parents divorce? Love the parent you're with, with all your heart. In other words, fill yourself with love for all who are with you now, this minute, this hour.

Better Relationships

Once a solid foundation is established in a relationship, what can the partners in the relationship do together spiritually to maintain balance between them even through tough times?

A relationship is like a garden in that both need constant attention. Both see days of sunshine and rain, which are necessary for produce and flowers to flourish. A garden also needs fertilizer and weeding.

Then, add lots of love. That will make for a wonderful and productive garden.

A relationship is therefore like a garden.

Each of the partners must sacrifice some freedom to the relationship. It means that both need to make changes, and that will draw power away from the ego. It means doing one's part, giving more than 50 percent to the relationship. It also means giving up habits that hurt it.

You said some key words in your question: "Once a solid foundation is established."

The point is that the job is never done. It needs tending all the time. Trouble often starts when one tries to tell the other what to do, even though the "good" advice is not asked for. If the one giving such advice persists despite clear signs that now is not the time or place for it, then it leads to heated words and hurt feelings.

One or both partners will have their blue, or down, days. The other must then show the wisdom and love to be more understanding than usual.

Love and gratitude for each other goes a long ways toward ensuring your happiness. Happiness, like heaven, must be rewon every day.

Love and gratitude for each other goes a long ways toward ensuring your happiness.

Being Gracious

One of my friends recently converted to Christianity, and I'm afraid this will deeply affect our relationship. I was always able to talk to her about religion before. All of my other Christian friends preach to me. As a result, I lose a close bond. Should I be concerned with such a change between me and my best friend?

These are among what could be either pleasant or uncomfortable changes in our lives. There are Christians and there are Christians. Just like ECKists.

Nobody with any degree of self-respect likes to be preached at, ECKist or Christian.

If she's really a good friend, her conversion will not stand in the way of your friendship. The first time a disagreement comes up between you on religion, say, "It's time we talk."

There's a saying: "Don't discuss politics or religion with friends unless they think like you." So agree on that.

Now remember, preaching at someone cuts both ways. Some ECKists make terrible pests of themselves at times too. Sad to say, in my exuberance at finding the ECK teachings years ago, I also plagued others with my excitement. No harm meant, but surely done. Of course, I paid dearly for that until it finally sunk in to keep my mouth shut.

The players in our life will include our best friends. How else could it be?

There's no reason to cry over spilled milk. It's the way of Soul's education here. The players in our life *will* include our best friends. How else could it be?

Some people are born with grace, wisdom, and a good measure of diplomacy. They can handle problems such as yours so that a friendship need not explode in your hands. There is a way to be gracious. It sometimes takes time for a friendship, a relationship, to right itself after a new spice is tossed into the pot.

Gaining Strength from Loss

I'm eleven years old, and my grandma died recently. That night, right before I went to bed, she came to my room as Soul. She called my name and said, "I love you. I will miss you. I am waiting for some more people to say good-bye to, and then I'm needed elsewhere." I miss her, and I'm really sad.

I'm also having a problem at school. I feel like I have no friends. My best friend betrayed me, and only one classmate will play with me at recess. I'm feeling so blue. What can I do?

Thank you for your thoughtful letter. Many of the problems of loss, betrayal, and some doubt about your self-worth have become less. The ECK, Holy Spirit, continues to guide your affairs in the direction that will help you most in a spiritual sense. Keep faith in the Mahanta, your inner guide.

Problems of one sort or another are always with us in some form or other. They are to make us strong. (Sometimes, though, we feel we're strong enough for now.)

Betrayal teaches us the pain of such an act. The lesson: not to betray another.

Loss can wound us deeply, but it will be with us from birth to translation (death). Lesson: to gain all the strength from it we can—then leave it behind and move on.

The ECK, Holy Spirit, continues to guide your affairs in the direction that will help you most in a spiritual sense.

Helping a Family Member

My older brother has been struggling for as long as I can remember with his spiritual path and himself. I see God giving him many gifts and experiences that he is blindly passing by.

I feel so helpless. I love him deeply, and I see how he hurts inside. What can I do to help him become happier with himself? Is there anything I can do to help him realize the experiences he goes through are great gifts that can guide him in the right direction?

Perhaps the hardest thing we face is seeing a loved one spurn life's blessings and choose the low road.

You'll see such behavior as long as you live. All you can do is give people like that your love, but not in a blind way. For example, if someone wants to harm himself with alcoholic drinks, illegal drugs, or even the purchase of material goods far beyond his means to afford them, think twice about being the moneybags.

So what's the issue here, his life or yours?

Right living also includes right discrimination. That boils down to having a command of our emotions. When a loved one chooses to walk the path of self-destruction, the choice is ours of how far we'll accompany him. That path will harm us too.

The big task in life is to keep our own life in order. That means controlling our runaway emotions.

The big task in life is to keep our own life in order. That means controlling our runaway emotions, for unless we do, the misguided steps of others will wreck our emotions.

It gets down to your choice. Will you let your older brother ruin both your lives? Keep in mind that the world is full of self-destructive people, but don't be a magnet for them. It's like trying to be a world savior. Adults are responsible for their own lives and must accept the consequences of their actions.

Yes, this is hard love. I wish this could be a

gentler answer, but life teaches many lessons through the deeds of others.

That lets us know that mud is dirty without soiling our own clothes.

Shielding Yourself

My ex-boyfriend used to drink from time to time, and when I would see him the next day, I would be affected by it. I know there was a strong bond between us since he was the man I loved, so his drinking would unbalance me. Can you tell me how I can shield myself against the secondhand effects of alcohol and drugs, please?

The only way to shield yourself is to get such things out of your life. But the choice is yours. Situations seldom are so cut and dried, though, especially when someone we love dearly suddenly takes up drinking, drugs, smoking, cursing, lying, or some other habit.

What do you do then?

An example from my own life with smoking: A friend of many years smokes several packs of cigarettes a day. Since last seeing him, I've become very sensitive to smoke. So when my friend wanted to visit me (the first time in over ten years), I had to tell him about my sensitivity.

We'd not be able to visit in a closed room. The smoke in his clothing would cause a serious health reaction for me. Believe me, it was a hard letter to send.

We remain friends. But all our correspondence must be in writing or by phone. Life gives us some hard choices.

The only way to shield yourself is to get such things out of your life. But the choice is yours.

Helping Youth in ECK

How can we help our children—and other ECK youth—as they grow and begin to wonder, Is this path the real truth? How can my parents be so sure about reincarnation, the ECK Masters, and the Far Country?

How would an ECK Master help the youth to become interested in doing the Spiritual Exercises of ECK?

Many longtime ECK members once had to fight major battles with family, friends, and clergy before they could follow ECK, the path of their choice. The strife made them tough.

In their darkest and loneliest hours, they found but one friend: the Mahanta. He was always there. They learned to have trust in the principles of ECK, which are stated in clear, open words in *The Shariyat-Ki-Sugmad*, Books One and Two. At least, those pure in heart will understand them.

Today sees a reversal of sorts. In the early days, seekers came from outside of Eckankar. Today, many of them have families, so their offspring are born inside the fold.

The challenge for ECK youth today is of a different sort.

The challenge for ECK youth today is of a different sort. They face the test *Is social acceptance worth more than the company of the Mahanta, the Living ECK Master?* They're on the outside of society's value system by birth. That's often a good reason to show contempt for all things of ECK, they feel. Their attempt at independence from parents' control may stretch to the ECK teachings.

They must work through this inner struggle. The teen years, in particular, are a time of strife and rebellion.

While on an errand yesterday, I met a woman whose gigantic dog stood guard at her side. But he was a gentle Soul.

"I raised him with gentleness," she explained. It showed.

No guarantees, but raise your children in like manner. It gives them every chance to weigh the value of rebellion against the bedrock of your love for them. Only the most willful child will toss such treasure aside.

Keep the Spiritual Exercises of ECK short, to fit the attention span of each child. Ask each to share inner experiences if so wished. And do family HU chants.

Best, show your love for your children. And for the spiritual exercises.

Raise your children with gentleness. Best, show your love for your children.

Children's Questions about God

How do you reply to a youngster who asks, "Who made God?"

"Go outside and play!"

If that doesn't work, you're in for it.

Young children often ask the most perplexing questions. In desperation I've resorted to, "Because!"

Because some things have no rational answer. And certainly, those matters that originate beyond the reach of man's pygmy mind, a denizen of the Mental Plane, a world below the true spiritual worlds, well—

There is no answer.

So how do you answer a child? Or an agnostic or atheist? The origin of God is beyond human understanding. Sugmad just IS.

*A child will
pick up on
love and
respect for
life and the
things of life.*

The only possible way to pass on even a shred of one's confidence in life in spite of not knowing the origin of our Creator is to do it via a bond of love. A child will pick up on a parent's love and respect for (1) the child, (2) other people, (3) animals, (4) plants, and (5) yes, even material goods that make life easier and more fulfilling. Love and respect for life and the things of life.

And, the child also learns by example and teaching that too much of a thing may be harmful. A wise parent demonstrates the way of moderation.

The existence of God, to a believer, is a matter of demonstration: the flower, the ant, the tree, sun, stars, water, air, etc. But the origin of God?

Your most honest answer is, "We don't know. We just know that God is love. Love has no beginning or end, and so neither does God."

Then kiss and hug your child and say, "God loves us, and I love you." It's the best answer of all.

Interracial Relationships

Growing up in Eckankar, I learned to love and view all people as Soul. Why do my parents object to my interracial relationship?

Sometimes parents are pointing out the extra cultural karma that their offspring may inadvertently take on in addition to the personal, family, and other karma that is part of any love relationship. Their opinion is to be considered carefully, of course, but the final decision is yours.

Everything depends upon the people, time, and place. If those three parts go against what a society accepts as normal, then members of that society will make life rough for the couple.

Let's draw a picture of an extreme case for you. Consider this: two people of the same sex *and* of mixed races who expect all the legal rights of a couple of opposite sexes. They would have a lot of problems in many parts of the world today. In a lesser way, a heterosexual couple of mixed races would have more problems in a lot of places than would a similar couple of the same race.

Weigh the odds and do as you please. It all adds to your spiritual unfoldment if you love one another.

It all adds to your spiritual unfoldment if you love one another.

Being Different

I am in fourth grade. People think I'm weird because of the way I look and my religion being ECK. It seems wherever I go to school people don't like me, and I have been to three schools. How come no one likes me? Why am I so different? Can you please help me through this?

Sometimes our schoolmates are cruel because we're new at a school and they're *afraid* something will be different for *them.* People really don't like change. It makes them feel unsure of themselves, so they pick on a new person at school.

Try to play down your differences. You may find it better not to tell others at school you are an ECKist. If the talk turns to religion, just say you believe in God and that you pray. Frankly, our religion is no one else's business but our own; of course, you can't just tell them so. Say you believe in God and that you pray. Leave it at that if you can.

Be friends with the ones who will be your friend. Be a *good* friend to them.

We choose our body and our parents before this lifetime. Your problems at school are making you self-reliant and strong. Put your efforts into your schoolwork. Also have a pet, if that's possible. My love is with you.

Being of Service to Others

My family decided to invite more people for the holidays than originally planned. I guess I am one of those people who just likes to spend the holidays with family, not twenty-one people.

My question is, should I feel so down when all these people are coming? Or am I being a little selfish?

Sometimes we just feel inadequate. I often did too. We feel as though the success of the party depends solely on us, and twenty-one people is far beyond our limit to serve and entertain by ourselves.

Ask your parents for a role at the party helping guests. Did you notice later how you ended up having a good time?

But no one expects that much of a thirteen-year-old girl.

Next time, ask your parents for a certain role at the party like serving soft drinks, helping young children find toys, or helping guests put away their coats upon arrival.

I used to fear the thought of parties too. But did you notice later how everything had a way of working out, so that you ended up having a good time?

Trust the Mahanta. Sing HU, the love song to God. And try to be of service to other people. Then things work out.

Intimacy and Karma

Do we take on the karma of an individual with whom we are intimate, even if there is not a marriage? And if so, how is this worked through by Soul?

Most certainly! While there may or may not be a problem with venereal diseases, there is surely the added complication of an emotional tie-in. Was your love finally rejected? Or did you reject another's love? Every relationship has an echo of sorts and will color your outlook, for good or ill, toward others.

Every relationship is based on karma. It may be one from the distant past or immediate present. All karma must be resolved, though.

This does not suggest that one is to avoid all relationships. But do make wise choices! After all, you will have to live with them as surely as the sun rises.

So many times I say, Be honest with yourself. Do your spiritual exercises. You *are* Soul! The exercises are your direct line to the Inner Master. He is the Wayshower, the one who can lead you safely through the minefields of life.

Every relationship is based on karma. It may be one from the distant past or immediate present.

Spirituality and Sex

My wife and I are going through changes the past few months. One outer manifestation has been that our sexual relationship, which used to be very beautiful and easy, has become a source of anxiety and insecurity. In the last few weeks we haven't been able to make love.

What does chastity mean? Is sexuality something that one has to leave behind in order to advance spiri-

tually? What is the highest spiritual purpose of a sexual relationship when it is no longer procreation?

Your letter has been much on my mind these past days. It is, of course, very unsettling when a beautiful and easy sexual relationship becomes a source of anxiety and insecurity because of an inability to make love. Where to start?

Chastity means to be pure in all your expressions of love for each other. Sexuality can become even more beautiful as a couple advances spiritually.

Chastity means to be pure in all your expressions of love for each other. Sexuality can become even more beautiful as a couple advances spiritually. The highest spiritual purpose of a sexual relationship is to share in the joy, love, blessings, and grace of divine love, whether it is for procreation or for showing love for one another.

Do explore possible health reasons and treatments for this recent inability to make love.

Another area to consider is the stress that could arise from your work. A good rule is to never bring business of any sort into the bedroom. It should be a place for rest and enjoyment, so leave work outside the bedroom door. Also get enough rest, especially a day or so before making love. You may want to plan ahead for a day of sexual love, but be willing to postpone that date if either of you has a health concern or some other unforeseen problem arises.

There are all sorts of self-help treatments on the market for the prostate, etc., but it's better to enlist the help of a good doctor of medicine or natural medicine.

Stress can be a real problem, so look closely in that area. Further, the body's fluids become less with age. It may take some attention to using supplemental fluids to help the body out.

Love makes you one. These general thoughts

should get you going in the right direction. You should have many happy years of lovemaking ahead of you.

Spiritual Impact of Sex Change

Since Soul is neither male nor female and may incarnate in a male body one lifetime and in a female body the next, I thought the process of gender reassignment, also called sex change, would not affect one's spiritual life in any deleterious way. But in reading passages in Paul Twitchell's The Tiger's Fang *about the female being of negative vibration and the male positive, and that only positive energy may enter the God Worlds, I begin to wonder. My wife and I were married in an ECK ceremony some years ago, and she was aware of my transgender status. From the spiritual standpoint, are we man and wife, or not?*

Your perception that a sex change in no way affects spiritual unfoldment is correct. Yes, you and your wife are married.

Please understand that Paul Twitchell had much to learn when he wrote his earlier books like *The Tiger's Fang*. God Consciousness had simply opened him to begin learning the finer points of the way spiritual principles work out in subtle manifestations.

As you can appreciate, your questions about the spiritual impact of a sex change do not come up routinely. So they allowed me to address them now.

Your perception that a sex change in no way affects spiritual unfoldment is correct.

What Is Love?

In the Eckankar book Stranger by the River, *by Paul Twitchell, what does it mean when the Tibetan*

ECK Master Rebazar Tarzs says that a woman's heart is the throne of God on earth?

The chapter is called "The Great Tree of Life." Read it very carefully again, from beginning to end. Rebazar Tarzs is comparing a life full of love to one without it.

Look especially at the paragraph before that, where he speaks of beauty. It is the harmony between joy and pain that begins in the body but ends beyond the mind. Beauty is "the power which leads man's heart to that of a woman, which is, on this earth, the throne of God."

Throne here means the source of divine love.

But Rebazar goes on, and what he says now is highly important, for it explains where true love begins and what conditions the lover must meet.

Love, says Rebazar, is "that holy liquor which God has wrung from His great heart and poured into the lover's heart for his beloved." Notice also the hint that not everyone can drink of this holy love, because the lover must meet a set condition: purity of heart. "He who can drink this liquor is pure and divine, and his heart has been cleansed of all but pure love!" That means, among other things, a lack of selfishness.

Open your heart to love, for it can help you reach the fullest satisfaction in life, with all its joy and pain.

Next, he speaks of the power of love in very powerful language: "Thus I say that the lover whose heart is drunk with love is drunk with God."

But Rebazar goes a step further. Love does not begin and end with one's love for his beloved, but it will of its own accord flow out to embrace all life. So his message is this: Open your heart to love, for it can help you reach the fullest satisfaction in life, with all its joy and pain. "Let this be thy understanding in Eckankar," he adds. "Share thy cup with thy beloved, and never fail to help thine own in pain and suffering. This should be thy law unto thyself, my son."

A final word: When Rebazar here speaks of man and woman, he doesn't only mean male and female, but the plus and minus sides of a human being. His message is about the power of love. This divine power can touch the heart in many ways, and love between a man and a woman is simply one of them.

I know this is a long reply, but perhaps it can point you toward a richer and happier life.

This divine power can touch the heart in many ways, and love between a man and a woman is simply one of them.

The Herd Instinct

Some youth feel they are missing something if they don't experience some of the things teenagers do (e.g., sex, drugs, rock and roll). What suggestions would you have to combat this peer pressure and keep your focus on God?

Average people try to pull exceptional people down to their own level. It's the herd instinct.

Prayer and Karma

I am frequently asked by Christians to pray for others, but I'm not sure what to do. They have these prayer chains that seem to have helped many in need. Can prayer affect karma or God's will in one's life?

Your question is about spiritual adolescence versus maturity. When others ask you to pray for others, it's with the idea that God hears the prayers of many petitioners better than the prayers of one. It's like God is an elected official.

Yes, prayer can affect karma in the short run. But

overall, the spiritual law of "payment in the true coin" prevails. Two points to consider: First, the healings are of a temporary nature (since even those whom Jesus once supposedly raised from the dead have long since died). Second, the group uses the healing, if any, as a control factor over the healed ("Out of gratitude, you should become a lifelong supporter of our group"). Where is the spiritual freedom?

Furthermore, these people are trying to rope you into their circle of control as well.

If someone is in need, they must ask for your help. You may also offer it. In any case, an offered prayer must be with the permission of the one in need. Members of a church usually give tacit agreement simply by being members there, because they know that's how that church does things.

Yet Soul's relationship with Divine Spirit is an individual one. We accept the fact of karma and reincarnation. A true Christian cannot. It's not a part of the Christian articles of faith. But all suffering is a repayment of an old karmic debt. The repayment of it brings about a degree of spiritual purification.

All this philosophy still leaves you wondering how to get along with your Christian friends. Arguing for or against a religious belief goes nowhere, because it's a strong emotional issue.

Choose your friends. Do they grant you as much spiritual freedom as you need?

The answer depends upon the situation.

A possible answer: "Don't you think God knows about the problem?"

In the end, choose your friends. There are many fine Christians who quietly follow their own beliefs without trying to force others to adopt them too. Other people are very pushy. You have to make the final decision about your own friends. Basically, do they grant you as much spiritual freedom as you need?

If not, it's time to find new friends.

Someone may ask for your prayers. In that case, say: "I will turn the matter over to Divine Spirit, because of myself I can do nothing." Then turn it over to the Mahanta, who will deal with it.

Your Family— Your Spiritual Choice

Did you spiritually choose me to be with a family in Eckankar, or was it random?

That's an interesting question. It's the same one that troubled me after coming into Eckankar, and many other young or new ECKists grapple with it. It applies to non-ECK families too.

Frankly, yours is another version of the question, "Are you really my parents? Or did you adopt me?"

If the question does come up, it's often when an individual is ten to fourteen. The child begins to have his own thoughts and opinions. Just as likely, he chafes at some duty or discipline from a parent to teach him the acceptable ways of the society he's born into. His education is the parent's responsibility, though.

Yet the youth sees longer and stronger feathers on his wings. (Or a boy may triumphantly spot a couple of long hairs on his chin, where he hopes the whiskers of manhood will soon sprout.) Maybe his feathers are long enough already to allow flights from the home nest? He thinks so.

That's where the question and a problem arise. His ideas, those of a fully dependent child, start to clash with those of his parent, whom divine law has

Yours is a version of the question, "Are you really my parents? Or did you adopt me?"

given the job of educator. The youth is becoming less dependent now.

So the youth, like a foolish fledgling, wants to *suddenly* be out on his own. But it's a cold, harsh world out there. Much harder than he's ready for.

To answer your question, the choice of your family was partly your own and partly your family's, and then approved by the Mahanta, the Inner Master, for spiritual reasons. This choice of family was not random.

Yes, you're in a good family. Since you're eleven, it will now take five to seven years for you to learn how to fully grow into the duties and responsibilities expected of you in our society. Your parents can make this transition easier on you. They've been around the block a few times. So listen and learn. The easy way.

True Self-Mastery

I read that ECK Masters enjoy life so much that they even risk being completely immersed in it. I would like to be deeply in love with life too. And yet I'm wondering how I can stand on my own feet spiritually and what I can do to actively strive for self-mastery in order to avoid being vulnerable when it comes to the loss of a love.

ECK Masters do love life so very much, even at the risk of being completely immersed in it.

The sad truth is that the loss of a love always leaves vulnerable the one whose idea it was that the love should have continued.

ECK Masters do love life so very much, even at the risk of being completely immersed in it. To survive, they surrender their whole being to the Sugmad and the ECK. When others turn from their love, they accept the fact and stand back, willing to let them be.

The Masters enjoy a full measure of divine love. When one beam of heavenly sunlight is shunted from them, they look to the rest of the light rays that do reach them, knowing that Sugmad's love is all around them still.

Absolute surrender to the divine will *is* true self-mastery.

Full surrender. It means a willingness to let new people and things into the circle of our personal area again. A new gift awaits our recognition of it.

Let the Mahanta guide you. You will find yourself in the happiest circumstances you could ever have dreamed possible.

First Step in Loving God

From a religious point of view, what is the importance of a physical relationship while obtaining spiritual freedom?

A loving relationship is the first step to loving God. Love unties the bonds that anchor us to the material world of wants and desires. So divine love leads directly to spiritual freedom.

The steps to spiritual freedom are these: (1) learn to love yourself, (2) learn to love others (human love), and (3) this will open your heart to love for God. That is the key to spiritual freedom.

Your journey to God begins at home.

A loving relationship is the first step to loving God. Your journey to God begins at home.

The high heavens are the true home of Soul. It is in exile in these lower worlds of time, space, and matter to learn the lessons of humility and love.

9
YOUR
PATH TO GOD

&ckankar states that it can lead one to the highest regions on the inner planes. Can this also be achieved on other paths?

Each path has a particular purpose as far as bringing a person to a certain level. And it isn't always the highest teaching within a path that comes forward to the people. The lower order of teachings in each group might say, "This is the highest path."

You have to remember, these are worlds God set up that are negative in nature so that Soul may develop Its spiritual qualities. The way the pattern of spiritual growth is set up, people learn more by the lessons they gain through hardship. Not through things they learn when life is easy.

I'm afraid we're all like that here. We enjoy life when it's easy, but that's not necessarily the time we learn our greatest spiritual lessons. We learn our best lessons when times are hard.

These are worlds God set up so Soul may develop Its spiritual qualities.

Why Are We Here?

*In the grand scheme of things, why are we here?
I believe I understand that we are here to attain Self-
Realization, then later God-Realization on our journey home to God to truly be a Co-worker. Why this
"journey" in the first place?*

Why this journey home to God?

Do you know the parable of the prodigal son? A
young man, born into all the advantages of a wealthy
family, decided to leave home and see the world.
Well, he wasted his money and ended up in a far
land, among strangers, working as a swineherd. He
would gladly have eaten what the pigs did.

One day it came to him: Here he was living
nearly like a beggar. Even his father's servants fared
better.

So the wastrel returned home.

"Father," he said, "I'm a waste. I'm not worthy to
be called your son. Make me as one of your servants."

But his father greeted him with joy and dressed
him in the finest clothes. Further, his father made
up a feast in celebration of his son's return home.

A beautiful story once told by Christ. He, like all
true avatars, told people of their divine heritage.
And so do we.

The journey to God is a journey back home to
God. The high heavens are the true home of Soul.
It is in exile in these lower worlds of time, space,
and matter to learn the lessons of humility and love.
Like the prodigal son.

On earth, the common state of awareness is the
human consciousness. As one learns more about
love and humility through the trials of many life-

*As one
learns more
through many
lifetimes,
he moves
higher in
consciousness.*

times, he moves higher in consciousness. First comes cosmic consciousness. Later, for one in ECK, Self-Realization and Spiritual Realization.

The highest level comes to the few who love and serve God with their whole being—God-Realization. It's a state of wonder and bliss beyond words. It's Soul's real destiny.

Now you know the story.

Spiritual Training

Where and how does the student of ECK receive his or her spiritual training?

The spiritual training for the ECK initiate begins *before* the person even becomes a member of Eckankar.

For instance, some people grow up as a member of a Christian group, like the Episcopal Church, and then, a few years later, they find that they are Lutheran perhaps. Then they'll go along a little farther, and find themselves a member of the Unity Church. And then as they progress in this life, after many hardships and experiences, they finally realize that they are looking for something else.

The religions of the past have not helped them fulfill the yearning for love, divine love, that's in their heart. And they come into ECK. Then they have taken the first big step in their journey back home to God.

The journey home to God is what life is about. In a sense it's not even a journey, it's an ongoing experience. But it does have to do with direction, because until a person finds the teachings of ECK, he is carried on a great wave from God that goes

The journey to God is what life is about.

all the way out into the universes.

As soon as you hear about ECK and accept its principles and teachings of divine love, you catch the return wave home. This is why it's such an important teaching for people who may come to the critical juncture in their life where they are serious about doing something more with their own life than they have been able to do so far on other paths.

Teachings of ECK Help People

How do the teachings of Eckankar help people?

The most important concept we need to get across is the *continuity of life*—going from this world to the next and beyond. People worry most about meeting the end of this life.

I mention this because of the illusion down here between this life and the next. Customs surrounding death vary from society to society, but most often the illusion of death is strong and causes fear.

The teachings of Eckankar are most helpful to people in presenting the continuity of life. It helps people lose fear. When you move from dream travel to Soul Travel, which is full consciousness, you become aware of having homes on these other planes of existence. You meet familiar loved ones there and other friends unknown to you here.

Soul shines the spotlight of consciousness on these higher areas of existence.

Doing the Spiritual Exercises of ECK is important because it clears out the impurities in the human consciousness that block awareness of the other planes. The ECK Masters bring the gift of the spiritual exercises so people may live more fully in God's

The ECK Masters bring the gift of the spiritual exercises so people may live more fully in God's love.

love. When God's love comes in, fear must go out—as do all the other passions of the mind.

The Spiritual Exercises of ECK put the mind in its place where it belongs, like a cart behind the horse. The mind may be a good servant, but it is a poor master.

The spiritual exercises keep the consciousness clear and your heart open to ECK, Divine Spirit.

Purpose of ECK Initiations

I haven't had an initiation in over ten years. I feel like I'm doing something wrong, but I don't know what. However, I feel like I've progressed spiritually over the years. How important are initiations? Are initiations different for youth than they are for adults? For example, do you have to be over eighteen to receive initiations above the Second Circle, and if so, why? What can one do to prepare for and achieve the next initiation?

It's generally true that one must be eighteen or older to get an initiation above the Second.

The reason is that experience in the physical life is a necessary part of spiritual unfoldment. Higher ECK initiations mean that a candidate has developed a greater sense of responsibility in all things. The greater responsibilities depend upon having a wide range of experiences—and dealing wisely with them.

Experience in the physical life is a necessary part of spiritual unfoldment.

Some people have a lot of experiences, but they are all of the same kind. They've learned nothing. All the lessons are simply a repeat of unlearned lessons with a new face. Like, twenty years spent learning the same thing, instead of learning twenty new things in twenty years.

In ancient Egypt, to cite one example, the mystery schools required years of study before a higher initiation took place. A youth—male or female— was carefully selected to attend those schools. He or she had to show a certain aptitude to start with. For example, a child might have had a history of prophetic dreams.

In ancient Egypt, a higher initiation meant leaving the love of one's family. Your training today comes in other ways.

That ability was only a first step to gaining admission to a mystery school. It also meant leaving the love of one's family. Homesickness was a real problem the youth needed to overcome. Some didn't. They washed out of temple training.

An active sex life was also out of the question. It also got in the way of training. So the individual had to redirect all his love to God during those years of training, which could amount to eight, twelve, or more years. That was the sort of responsibility required of someone in training for higher initiations in ancient Egypt.

Today we see an "instant meal" society. However, the spiritual standards of responsibility and self-discipline are the same. One's unfoldment cannot be popped into a microwave oven for quick initiations. But stick with it. Your training today comes in other ways.

Uprooting the Ego

I feel my ego is quite large. I have a really hard time trying to get rid of it. How can I know what my true destination as Soul is and not be misled by my ego? How can I distinguish between ego and Soul and make decisions Soul-wise and not ego-wise?

Many people have a hard time telling the difference between the two, so don't despair. Fortunately, you have an edge on them.

What's responsible for not being able to clearly see the difference between Soul guidance and ego guidance? The blinders of the Kal (negative power). What's his interest in this? He wants to see people unhappy, which comes of their making wrong choices. Unhappiness, then, is the result of taking advice from the ego, a tool from Kal's workshop.

Mental determination will not unseat the ego. They're tools from the same shop. So what can uproot the ego?

Something from the Mahanta's workshop. In a word, love.

Here you may want to read *Stranger by the River* by Paul Twitchell, and carefully read chapter 8 on love. Then skim other chapters. Look for all references to love.

Only divine love can conquer the ego. All else will fail.

The best way to attune yourself to guidance from Soul is to do every little and big thing in the name of the Mahanta. Then be confident in your decisions. You will very quickly find that wrong choices will grow fewer, even as you surrender a few coins to the tollgate of experience.

That's the reason for planet Earth. It's God's garden for Soul to get enough experience. Then Its choices will, more often than not, line up with those of the ECK, Divine Spirit.

You will very quickly find that wrong choices will grow fewer, even as you surrender a few coins to the tollgate of experience.

Soul Travel

Why is there such a focus on Soul Travel, and what is it?

Soul Travel has its range of experience. Some people notice it as just a shift in consciousness. All of a sudden something happens in their lives where they become aware they understand something they haven't before.

It comes in like a soft, golden kiss of God. Then they just *know* something.

Soul Travel can also be a stronger experience where people are actually lifted completely out of the body and they have some experience in the other worlds. It depends upon what they're ready for, what's necessary for their spiritual unfoldment.

Surrendering to God

You've written about the "eye of God." While surrendering to the will of God, I was standing in the middle of a pyramid of pure white light with the eye hovering over the top. There were patches of light missing, and it was a little dim until I put my attention on the love of God. Then the pyramid was complete and brilliant.

I was puzzled because it reminded me of the symbol on an American dollar bill, except my pyramid was white and the eye was above it. I thought this symbol was psychic, but my experience felt deeply spiritual. Any comments on this symbol?

This experience was of a spiritual nature, of course. First, it was a regular, not inverted, pyramid. Second, it was of pure white light. Third, the eye of God hovered over it.

The pyramid is a symbol for the whole unit of your being. Each face of a pyramid has three sides, and three is the creative number of Soul. Yet the foundation of a square pyramid, which we're interested in, is a four-sided structure. Four is the number of stability. Four plus three equals seven, "by which the divine law manifests itself in seven major aspects in the worlds of God" (*The ECK-Vidya, Ancient Science of Prophecy,* p. 141).

In brief, though, this triangle signifies divine love.

Patches of divine light are missing in your life until you put your full attention upon the Sugmad (God). Then the pyramid, and your joy and fulfillment in life, is complete.

Protection from Illusion

I have heard that the kabbalah can be used to change one's name so as to have a balance in the lower worlds. Could this be helpful to someone in ECK?

The teachings of ECK transcend the psychic teachings, which mislead Soul by putting attention upon the phenomenal instead of the substantial ECK doctrines.

Our names at birth fit our spiritual development as does the family into which we are born. There is no advantage in changing names when spiritual unfoldment occurs, because this could occur every few months.

The Mahanta protects the spiritual student from lower-world illusions.

Changing names to fit kabbalistic thought has no more validity to an ECKist than does astrology upon the direction of his future. The Mahanta works in the pure spiritual worlds and protects the chela (spiritual student) from lower-world illusions of this sort.

Spiritual Realization

In The Holy Fire of ECK, *Book 2, you write briefly about Spiritual Realization, a state between Self-Realization and God-Realization, "which is somewhere between the Fifth and the end of the Sixth, Seventh, and Eighth Initiations." Can you share some insights on this state of realization? Can you say more about what characterizes Spiritual Realization?*

There will be few outer signs. The changes will be in the heart. A veil will pull aside.

To a casual observer, there will be few outer signs. The changes will be in the heart. Only the Mahanta will see them in whole.

However, the individual who stands upon the threshold of Spiritual Realization will be refined in character. It's somewhat like a music lover whose appreciation for music evolves to an embracing of Beethoven or Mozart, giants in classical music.

Is there a way to explain the sensitivities of such a devotee of music to someone who loves pop music?

In other words, the benefits of Spiritual Realization are of a highly refined kind. Yet for all that, they are a precursor to God-Realization, even as the Fourth Initiation is to the Fifth Initiation. But a lot more so.

I suggest you read *The Shariyat-Ki-Sugmad* for all it says about Self-Realization and God-Realization.

Hold this body of knowledge lightly in hand, take it to the Mahanta in your contemplations, and ask him to fill in the blanks between them. You will, in time, notice a subtle shift to a higher level. Your spiritual senses will be refined. The outer and inner experiences will take on a new light.

A veil will pull aside.

Your heart will find a new level of peace, love, and joy. That's all that can be said about Spiritual Realization at this time. However, the quest is worth the effort.

Our Spiritual Unfoldment

Why do longtime chelas (spiritual students) of Eckankar leave the path?

This answer may seem funny at first glance, but it's a fact of Eckankar being around longer and longer. Longtime chelas leave the path because Paul Twitchell brought out the ECK teachings in 1965. To put this into a perspective, nearly none of the original followers of Eckankar are around any longer. The reason is that many of them melted away in the early years, while others have dribbled away since then. Others translated (died).

Most leave because they've forgotten their experiences with the Sound and Light of ECK. Usually, more to the point, today's experiences are of a different sort than those on the Astral Plane in the early years and now lack the luster of those sparkling and glimmering times.

But sparkle and glimmer remain still today for those initiates who continue with their spiritual exercises, while going through the dark zone that separates their present plane of consciousness from the one above. That may take days, months, or years. It all depends upon their desire for God—how strong is it? If in their hearts they're at the Astral, Causal, or Mental states of consciousness, they will make less and less of an effort to go beyond there.

It all depends upon their desire for God— how strong is it?

For example, a Fourth Initiate may feel comfortable at the Mental Plane but push on into the Fifth Plane, to become a dweller on the threshold there. He gets the Fifth Initiation but gets tired of the spiritual exercises. So he doesn't do them, or he does them with a halfhearted effort. No surprise, then, that nothing happens. So eventually he leaves the path of ECK, again. No problem. That happens to chelas many times in their spiritual unfoldment.

Out here in the human world, though, their leaving is a shock and a test for their friends. Ecclesiastes: There is no new thing under the sun. Indeed, there isn't.

Kal's Gardeners

Why do people (some who have never really been in Eckankar, and even some High Initiates) leave Eckankar and then go and write books bashing the ECK teachings? Why do they do this? What do they get spiritually out of these negative thoughts and actions?

There is an upside to it.

It could be a disturbing thing but it's not—at least not to me. There is an upside to it. But let's cover that in a moment.

The *downside* all falls to the Judas, the one who betrays a sacred trust once made to the Mahanta, the Living ECK Master. The agreement runs like this: You may become a disciple of ECK if you vow never to turn another's face from the Light and Sound of ECK.

People come and go in Eckankar; that's understood. But it's a violation of spiritual law to mislead even one seeker, because then one's unfoldment in ECK this lifetime is at an end.

These betrayers of ECK will pick up all their old karma once more. More, the karma of all those whom they've fooled is inscribed into their karmic log too.

Hard, hard times lie in store for them.

Yet there is also an *upside*, though it may seem to be of a doubtful sort.

It is this: Only those who are weak in the spiritual principles can be fooled. They are weeds among vegetables. In this case, the gardener is an agent of Kal, who'll use every trick in his gardener's apron to rid the ECK garden of all who do not belong there.

So you see, there's no concern in the long run about such lost Souls. It's because no Soul is ever lost. Such a thing is impossible. ECK is the lifeline for all things.

All, and everybody, is in life's ordered universe.

No Soul is ever lost. Such a thing is impossible. ECK is the lifeline for all things.

A Foil for Every Segment of Truth

What about writings that attack the authenticity of Eckankar?

One former strong critic has stopped attacking the ECK teachings, even though his writings remain on the Internet. In fact, he now quietly supports us.

Yet Eckankar will always have detractors, since that is part of the educational system here.

Oddly enough, the pattern of the negative worlds requires that truth be pelted from all sides. There must be a foil for every segment of truth on earth, because otherwise it could not exist below the Fifth, or Soul, Plane.

Everything down in the spirito-material worlds

requires the balance of its opposite for survival. The enigma of all this is that Soul recognizes the importance of the negative power as the educator or teacher, but It strives anyway to rise above restrictions of any kind in spiritual things.

The point of any saint or teaching is: Can this lead anyone to the Light and Sound of God?

The point of any saint or teaching is: Can this lead anyone to the Light and Sound of God?

Written words derive from a place no higher than the Mental Plane, because that is the source of the alphabet, symbols, and thought. The Essence of God, the ECK, has at that point just made Its incursion into the realm of negativity from the indescribable worlds of God above.

More information is coming out all the time about people who have reported meeting ECK Masters, like Rebazar Tarzs, before they had even heard of Eckankar.

I've included detailed accounts of many people's meetings with these ECK Adepts in my book *Those Wonderful ECK Masters*. Or see *ECK Masters and You: An Illustrated Guide* for a shorter introduction to these Co-workers with God and how they can help you.

Yes, everything is in order.

Finding a Comfortable Relationship with the ECK

Something about your eyes makes me feel that I know you. When I began reading the ECK books, I felt as though I'd literally been dropped into place. Everything I had ever thought or believed in was right there. The joy I felt was so great, I cried tears of joy.

The path of ECK is the most direct route to the highest experiences of God. Please take your time with this study. If one can find love, peace, and balance in daily life, he or she has the blessings of God.

Most people who desire God look for the God State too far from home, but the seed of spiritual greatness is in the heart of all. The spiritual exercises help one find a comfortable relationship with the ECK, the Holy Spirit—and so with all life.

God's Love Strengthens

My husband is a retired Episcopal priest, and I have been a lifelong Christian and devout Episcopalian. I've learned about Eckankar and see my spiritual growth, but I feel at a standstill, with one foot on the Christian path and one foot on the path of ECK.

Thoughts of having to resign from my church and depart from the Christian faith make me feel as if I am standing on the edge of a cliff, trembling in fear.

If it will ease your mind, you do not have to resign from your church to follow the ECK teachings. You can follow and love ECK no matter what your other religion may be.

You can follow and love ECK no matter what your other religion may be.

There is no need to create such a hardship for yourself and your family, because God's love strengthens good families and relationships instead of splitting them up. In the end, though, the decision is your own.

Keep kindness and love for others in mind, and all will be well.

ECK Disciplines

In the Eckankar books I read about self-discipline, true contemplation of the ECK works, and complete inner reliance on the Mahanta. What do these terms really mean?

Sometimes people (and you) see yourself as going against the grain. You too often like to do it your way, regardless of the thoughts and feelings of others.

Such a budding independence of thought occurs to many of us at your age. We know a little and jump the gun. It's perfectly obvious to us, at age fifteen, that we know it all and should have a bigger role in decisions that affect us. That's all fine, but isn't it the ego on a rampage? Much trouble lies down that road.

So how does an ECK chela tie in self-discipline to true contemplation?

A daily contemplation (it only has to be five minutes at bedtime or upon arising) can control a wild ego, our little self. The spiritual exercise can help you learn the ways of ECK in our world. That includes learning what's right or wrong.

A daily contemplation at bedtime or upon arising can control a wild ego, our little self.

Then what does complete inner reliance on the Mahanta mean?

The short spiritual exercises done twice a day will slap a bridle on a runaway, wild ego. In plain language you can learn to admit to wrong thoughts and opinions. It's a big step. Then the Mahanta's voice can come through the fog of your human consciousness to show you an easier way in your spiritual life.

So self-discipline is the key to a spiritual life. It's the gateway to a true contemplation of the ECK works.

That, in turn, lets you hear the Mahanta's voice.

You correctly named the three key parts to leading a true spiritual life. But now the ball's in your court.

God Qualities

I do not understand animals killing each other cruelly in the jungle. If I was God and was all knowing, all seeing, and all powerful, why would I create a Soul which would need all these ugly experiences? Instead, I think I would create a world in which everybody is happy and knows all, without need for suffering. Please tell me why a "Loving Father" has such a gloomy plan.

In the pure world of Soul there is no death. Birth and death are both illusions of these lower worlds of matter, energy, space, and time. God put Soul in that perfect heaven above the Soul Plane, but It wasn't developing the God qualities of love and mercy.

So God created the lower worlds out of spiritual necessity. Each Soul was sent there to become more godlike in nature.

This process of karma and reincarnation is like the mill wheel that grinds exceedingly fine. Like it or not, that is the divine plan.

Yours is a good and honest question. The fact is that on our way to becoming a Co-worker with God, we do actually get a chance to create our worlds as we see fit. In everyday terms, it means we can make our home as pleasant as heaven. That means, of course, that we have to be pleasant too.

Put all God qualities like patience and love together in yourself, and you will be a joy to all who know you. In fact, you'll be one of those saints spoken of with reverence in the histories of religions.

Put all God qualities like patience and love together in yourself, and you will be a joy to all who know you.

The Power of HU

What would you recommend a person do to prove the authenticity of the path of ECK?

I would suggest to sing the word *HU*. If you are going to have success on this path at all, generally you'll get it by singing HU. The way to sing HU is in a very long, drawn-out breath. Sing the word just simply as *HU-U-U-U*.

Sing this song either silently or softly in prayer or meditation sessions for ten to fifteen minutes a day for a month. Try it this way. Then if nothing happens, give yourself a rest for a month or two. Later, if you remember, do it again. If nothing happens, don't worry about it, because when the seeker is ready, the Master appears. It's spiritual law.

When you're ready, you're going to find your next step on the spiritual path.

Customizing Your Spiritual Exercises

I am a dancer, and I wonder if there could be (or ever has been) Spiritual Exercises of ECK in movement? I know about the systems like yoga, tai chi, or certain forms of martial arts, but they seem to be rooted in other spiritual paths and therefore appear not to aim at experiences with the pure Light and Sound. Is this possible with physical exercises, or do they just aim for physical health (or art, as in dance)?

The whirling dervishes of Persia, a Muslim sect, danced until reaching a trance state, where they enjoyed the bliss of Allah. Their dance was a spiritual exercise.

Neoplatonists of ancient Greece, followers of

Plato, felt that a sacred dance would allow for the sudden arrival of God, who'd then take part. Whatever the sacred dance, it was often performed in a circle around a center, to show how all life revolves around the Creator.

It's well to remember that ECK is the origin of all religions. Many ECK chelas were once members of them in past lives, so it's understandable that you and other dancers may wish for a spiritual exercise in a dance form.

Why not develop your own?

Keep in mind that a spiritual dance will bring a dancer into harmony with the rhythm of the divine Sound Current. It's a dance to open the heart. It will bring joy and produce a spirit of thanksgiving for the gift of life. And look for the dance to change.

Begin with a simple dance. The Mahanta will reveal new steps and movements as you unfold spiritually in your efforts to become one with ECK, the Holy Spirit.

A spiritual dance will bring a dancer into harmony with the rhythm of the divine Sound Current.

Experiences with the Mahanta

If you have an experience with the ECK (Holy Spirit) or the Light and Sound, is that an experience with the Mahanta? Is there a difference? When Saul of Tarsus had an experience with the Light, did he have an experience with the Mahanta?

It depends upon whether the individual is on the path of ECK or on another path. In ECK, the manifestations of the Light and Sound are connected with the Mahanta, the Living ECK Master. For an individual on another path to God, these manifestations appear through the incarnation or image of that path.

Everything depends upon the individual's state of consciousness.

Light and Sound exist everywhere, on each plane. However, the vibrations of the Light and Sound, as those of Its chief agent for a spiritual path, do vary a lot—from the highest to many degrees of lesser vibrations.

Everything, of course, depends upon the individual's state of consciousness.

Sometimes the ECK Masters approach someone like Saul (later St. Paul) to begin a mission of great spiritual importance. Paul was to be the spark plug who would spread the teachings of Christianity far and wide. The consciousness of people was ready for a new step. His message in large part abandoned the God of Fear so predominant in the Old Testament. He preached about the God of Love. Divine love was the original focus of Christianity—a startling concept in those primitive times.

Also remember that a special messenger like Paul doesn't just happen. Before that lifetime, he was chosen by the spiritual hierarchy for that mission. Not only that, he accepted it.

The Light of God on the road to Damascus was simply his wake-up call.

And, yes, the ECK Master Zadok was an early influence upon Paul.

Becoming Self-Reliant

How can people become self-reliant and independent when Divine Spirit controls everything?

That's a very good question.

Spirit, however, does not control everything. Sure, It is life itself—to that degree, yes. But providing life is not the same thing as living each individual's life.

Let's look at it like this:

Say, Spirit (the ECK) is like your home. It provides shelter, but whatever you do inside is left pretty much up to you—except for the house rules of your parents. So, too, does the ECK provide you with life. But there are rules, spiritual laws, that are a part of living.

Now here's where the play of free will comes in. You have the choice of following or breaking the rules—all, some, or none of them.

There are rules, spiritual laws, that are a part of living. Now here's where the play of free will comes in.

Let's see two possible ways of regarding our life. We may think of it as either a trial or an opportunity. Those two ways of looking at life also apply to each and every thing that happens to us. For example, you throw a ball wild and it breaks a window. You learn quickly not to do that again.

That's the bad part.

But if you can learn to be careful in other things and not be careless and break something, your life will turn a corner and be more pleasant in a lot of other ways.

Yet here the play of free will comes in. What happens if you stand in the same spot as before and throw the ball?

Right, there's a good chance you'll learn the no-no's of doing that again.

So learn and obey the spiritual laws early. Life is more pleasant then.

Born into ECK

I read in Wisdom of the Heart, *Book Two, that new ECKists get a dream from you, the Mahanta, that signifies their first initiation. What happens to those born into ECK, such as myself?*

It's a good question. The quote you refer to is: "[The] First Initiation . . . comes in a dream during the first year *or so* (italics added) of study in the ECK works."

Yes, it's as your question suggests. For some, especially those who are born into ECK, the inner Dream Initiation could come much later, when they are spiritually ready for it.

If we wish to speak of *grace*, it might apply in cases where a Soul is born into an ECK family and may even receive the Second Initiation while still an infant. This "grace" part means that the child is then also under the Master's protection, since through its birth into the ECK family it agreed to his spiritual protection.

A spiritual rule to keep in mind is this: No one else can enter heaven for you.

There is a spiritual rule, though, to keep in mind. It is this: No one else can enter heaven for you.

One's birth into an ECK family may provide all the advantages of spiritual unfoldment, but that's not to say that Soul will appreciate them. The Kal, or negative power, will do all it can to exploit the passions of an individual to keep him in spiritual slavery.

That's the seemingly endless cycle of births and deaths.

Yes, some people who were born into ECK families have slipped from the path. But that's their problem.

When you're ready, you'll clearly remember your First Initiation. But a hint: It may be a dream experience that occurs periodically over a period of days, weeks, months, or even years. Yet in the whole, it is one event, your First Initiation.

This life has so many riches to offer, but choose wisely. And always keep my love for you in mind.

Rite of Passage

In Eckankar, the ECK Rite of Passage is one of the celebrations of life. What does this ceremony mean spiritually? How do you know when it is time to receive your Rite of Passage? Is there a recommended age range for it?

The ECK Rite of Passage is one of the celebrations of life. It celebrates a new stage in Soul's journey home to God. Namely, it marks a person's growth from childhood to the threshold of becoming an adult.

This ceremony is for a youth who wants to begin taking on more responsibility in life, as well as for making a personal commitment to the ECK teachings. And to accepting the Mahanta for one's spiritual guide.

Around age thirteen or so is generally the time for this celebration of life, but one may take it to perhaps age twenty-one.

A youth who wishes to celebrate the ECK Rite of Passage needs to know the basic teachings of ECK. You or your parents can get more information about that from any member of the ECK clergy.

You'll know when you're ready for it. Then ask.

The ECK Rite of Passage celebrates a new stage in Soul's journey home to God.

God-Realization

Other religions group together cosmic consciousness and God-Realization as the same experience. Eckankar states that there is, in fact, a difference. How can we tell them apart?

Cosmic consciousness is directly connected with the Mental Plane. It comes from the mental region where all our thought, philosophy, logic, and various arts along this line, such as mathematics, come from. Cosmic consciousness is the high part of the mental region and it gives primarily the Light of God but not the Sound.

Someone who had the experience of cosmic consciousness came to me to ask whether this was God Consciousness, and I didn't answer the person, because I can't. If someone has to ask, it isn't.

If you have God Consciousness, you don't have to tell anyone, outside of my role because it's my duty to do so. It's the duty of the spiritual leader of the teachings of ECK to announce himself and make the path of spiritual wisdom freely available to other people. So all those who are ready can find their way to it, so that I can help them put all their attention and efforts toward rising to a higher place of existence than the physical.

Brothers of the Leaf

Can you tell me more about the High Initiates in Eckankar and why they are called the Brothers of the Leaf?

The Brothers of the Leaf are like leaves on the same tree, the ECK.

The Brothers of the Leaf are mentioned but once in *The Shariyat-Ki-Sugmad.* They are the Mahdis, those who have reached the Fifth Initiation.

As *The Shariyat* says, it is a small band of people with strong spiritual ties. And like the Three Musketeers of literary fame, they act as one for all and all for one. They are like leaves on the same tree, the ECK.

They have a secret internet of communication with each other. So they can talk via the inner net.

A Mahdis can also be said to have turned a new

leaf. His view of living and of this world underwent a complete transformation at the Fifth Initiation. In fact, it's hard for a Mahdis to even remember the confused and troubled state of mind he carried before then.

And yet, as with everything in a spiritual sense, heaven must be rewon every day.

It means that an ECK initiate, even a Mahdis or higher, must take heed lest he fall.

More could be said about the Brothers of the Leaf, but a true understanding of that band occurs when one becomes a member of it. Only a Mahdis can understand his new freedoms and joys.

Keep on with the ECK teachings, and your day will come too.

Initiation Signposts

ECK initiations are "markers" on our way home to God. Within higher initiations, when there are few strong inner experiences, what are some signposts we could be looking for as signs of our progress on the path?

Signs of our progress on the path are as unique as is each Soul.

The signposts for these spiritual markers can be just about anything. They are as unique as is each Soul. The Mahanta will show you what's necessary.

It is true that a Higher Initiate may have few strong inner experiences of the kind that used to fill his inner life. Dreams, Soul Travel, visions, and snapshots of the past or future may be fewer, but there are new signposts. You must learn to see them.

How? you may well ask. How can I see or know what I can't see or know? A catch-22.

Believe it, you can. Once you know it's possible to see and learn the spiritual signposts of the higher, more subtle kind, you'll begin to see them. It's no different at all from the step-by-step abilities you once developed to learn the secrets of dreams, Soul Travel, and other signposts.

Everything is possible in a spiritual sense. Since your growing awareness let you clearly see your problem of the difficulty in recognizing higher spiritual markers, the new awareness will come too.

Here again, the key is the Spiritual Exercises of ECK. They've brought you this far. They are the Mahanta's gift to help you on your way home to God. Do them with joy and expectation.

What Is the Light and Sound?

The Light and Sound are the two aspects of God that speak to the human race, that speak to each Soul.

Eckankar is defined as the Religion of the Light and Sound of God. What is the Light and Sound?

The Light and Sound are the two aspects of God that speak to the human race, that speak to each Soul. The Light and Sound together are the Voice of God, what the Old and New Testaments call the Holy Spirit or the Logos. Together they are simply divine love.

Ups and Downs
of the True Spiritual Path

I've just recently read the book ECKANKAR—Ancient Wisdom for Today. I'm seventeen years old, and I've had questions about my spiritual growth and about God. After reading this book, I figured I was on the right track, though.

I feel it's the right thing to do to meet life head-on and try to learn from it. But I've had hard ex-

periences like getting an abortion and learning too late how much I loved a special man in my life. I hope I'm not burdening you, but I felt I had to write you to get it all out.

Thank you for your letter. I'm glad you liked *ECKANKAR—Ancient Wisdom for Today*. It simply tries to show what a person can expect in the way of spiritual freedom and what one needs to do to earn it. Many of the people in ECK are strong individuals. They want to know things for themselves.

You'll find that a true spiritual path is a lot like a relationship; it has its ups and downs. Mainly, the ups and downs all begin within ourselves. The world only reflects who and what we are. But that's OK. After all, the nature of truth is not always to be pretty and easy—otherwise more people would have it.

The people who use the ECK teachings for a guideline to run their lives are unique, strong, and independent types. ECK lets you learn through the outer and inner teachings both. Very different and exciting.

However you decide to go in the future, be yourself.

Led to the Path

I've just come across the ECK teachings, and one of your books so powerfully expressed what I have been looking for all my life. I feel drawn to serving others and want to be a Co-worker with God. Once I had an incredible experience with the Light. I think it may have been a glimpse of the wonder of God.

Have I been led to follow this path?

The path to God is always a serious undertaking. The Spirit of Life (the ECK, Holy Spirit, etc.) will

ECK lets you learn through the outer and inner teachings both. Very different and exciting.

This purification brings about a new ability to see and experience the causes in life.

demand everything from you. Then It gives it all back. The process of cleaning is very thorough: from attic to basement. This purification has a purpose, of course. It's to lift the individual in his state of consciousness, which brings about a new ability to see and experience the causes in life. All causes ultimately spring from divine love. I'm not merely using words here, but I think you understand that from your own past spiritual experiences.

It is physically possible to do only so much as the Outer Master (write letters, etc.), but as the Inner Master there are no limits. So we can begin to meet in the dream state, if you wish.

Working Consciously with the Masters

I want to consciously work with the Masters, but I'm uncertain. How do the Mahanta and the Masters of the Vairagi fit into the hierarchical order with the angels, the White Brotherhood, Jesus, etc.?

Even though I'm a High Initiate in ECK, I find myself in another doubting stage. I need clarity on these matters to serve and grow spiritually. Please be direct with me.

The experiences of a High Initiate will not be like the phenomenal ones of circles one through three. Each step higher calls for more self-reliance, less dependence upon anyone or anything—except for the ECK and the Mahanta. They are always with you.

About the spiritual hierarchy: the answers are in Books One and Two of *The Shariyat-Ki-Sugmad* as well as in *The Spiritual Notebook*. A careful review will also restore a conscious link with the Mahanta, should you wish to do so.

The spiritual basics need to be reviewed, especially within a year or two of your twelve-year anniversary of the Second Initiation. Unless you go back and review the basics of ECK, your doubts will run away with you. You'll end this life pretty much at the same place at which you were spiritually before joining ECK. I hope this helps.

Blue Star of ECK

In contemplation, and after a major realignment of my heart with the Mahanta, I saw a large, beautiful six-pointed white star with perfect clarity. What does it mean? I had been used to the Blue Star of ECK, but somehow this was different. Also, can you tell me about the six-pointed star in the Temple of ECK?

The Blue Star of ECK is a manifestation of the Mahanta to chelas usually before the Fifth Initiation. However, a Mahdis, a High Initiate, may continue to see the Blue Star too.

The Blue Star of ECK means the presence of the Mahanta.

A six-pointed white star means the presence of the Mahanta as it appears to an initiate on the Soul Plane or higher.

The six-pointed star in the ECK Temple is significant because it is connected with the high path of ECK, whether blue, white, yellow, pink, orange, or golden.

What's Different about Eckankar?

There are so many choices available to the seeker of truth today, including various teachings of the

Light and Sound. What makes Eckankar different?

There aren't that many teachings about the Light and Sound. There are a lot of teachings that know nothing about either the Light or the Sound as an important part of the spiritual path.

Christianity speaks about the Light in a number of places in the Scriptures. For instance, Saul on the road to Damascus—that was the Light of God. I don't think Christianity understands the full importance of the Light of God. And even those religions that do have both the Light *and* Sound of God may not fully understand the importance of having both of them as part of a viable spiritual path.

So, in ECK we teach that there is this balance of the two aspects so people can have the straightest, most direct, and most spiritually beneficial path to God.

Path to Mastership

You become an ECK Master through love and love alone. It's all about love for God.

How do you become an ECK Master?

Through love and love alone.

However, it is anything but a love without aim or direction. It's all about love for God.

Striving for ECK Mastership is certainly a worthy goal.

Above all, do what you love, and love what you do. That sounds like the same thing said twice. It's not.

All the things we do won't be of our choosing. Otherwise, we'd avoid the very things which we need to do in order to learn some important lessons. There will be many such occasions.

Then, love what you do.

And do your very best no matter what. A way to tell a person with a far-advanced state of consciousness is to notice the way he tries to do everything with excellence—but always with love. No shortcuts! That means learning patience too.

It took me many years to learn patience, but the ECK Masters put me in one situation after another. Finally, over time, the lessons took hold.

The ideas here will stand you in good stead, whether or not you decide to try for the ECK Mastership.

A good primer for mastership I highly recommend is my book *Autobiography of a Modern Prophet*. It will help you travel your own path to God.

Remember, love and love alone.

Do your very best no matter what—but always with love.

The spiritual purpose of life is to learn to give and receive divine love.

10
SERVICE TO ALL LIFE

What is the spiritual purpose of life?

It's to learn to give and to receive divine love.

Keeping the Heart Open

I have trouble keeping my heart open sometimes. Do you have any advice for me?

You're not alone. It is very hard to keep your heart open today. The world sometimes spins a lot faster than we can run to keep up. Especially in school.

Others go out of their way to hurt us and cause trouble. That pressure makes it harder to keep up with the work in class or to fit in with classmates. There are a lot of big questions about the future too. At this moment, you stand on the threshold between your childhood and adult years. A time of change, for sure.

To keep your heart open, do one small, unsung good deed every day.

Little things now will tend to blow up, or exaggerate, in importance. So these otherwise minor points will try to create monsters out of mice. More than ever, look to the Mahanta for love.

There is one last thing. To keep your heart open,

do one small, unsung good deed every day in the Mahanta's name. I am always with you.

The Secret of Service

What is the secret of service?

In a word, love.

The path to it starts with the Mahanta, the Living ECK Master.

The path connects to the ECK Audible Life Current (Holy Spirit) through him. He guides the chela into the heart of God.

Thereupon the chela becomes a Co-worker with God. *The Spiritual Notebook* by Paul Twitchell says, "He will dwell in eternity in peace and happiness."

You see, service to God is a natural outcome for all who do the Spiritual Exercises of ECK every day. They learn to travel in the other worlds. There they find the spiritual benefits of ECK, which are "companionship, life, hope, love, peace, and self-reliance." The last chapter of *The Spiritual Notebook* tells of that.

Service to others is a natural outpouring of one's love for life.

So service to others is a natural outpouring of one's love for life. I hope this answers your question.

God's Missionaries

What is the difference between the Vahana (missionary) work we do in Eckankar and the missionary work we know from other religions?

A missionary has a message and wants to tell others about it.

But there are religions and there are religions. There are missionaries and there are missionaries.

There are messages and there are messages.

In general, though, several forces may drive a missionary, like fear, greed, lust, attachment, and vanity. Did you notice that these are our old friends, the passions of the mind? They tend to show up in the oddest places.

Fear of his Lord's rebuke on Judgment Day may drive a Christian missionary. He believes it's his duty to ensure that family and friends are of his religion and remain so.

Greed may power one's ardor. Let's say someone has started a new church and his salary depends upon gathering a large flock. Also, lust is along the same lines. The missionary delivers his message for selfish reasons if, say, he wants to gain influence over an attractive woman.

Attachment plays out a bit like fear. The missionary, for family or group security, wants to convert and keep all within his sphere of influence. Vanity, too, can show up, perhaps, in the head counter. It flatters him to be the missionary who netted the most new converts to his church.

However, love is greater than all the mind passions combined. An ECK Vahana or a missionary of any other religion who is a carrier of God's *pure* love has no base motives and his message has no strings attached. This messenger loves goodness and charity, and his missionary work shows it.

A carrier of God's pure *love has no base motives.*

Answering "What Is Eckankar?"

When people ask, "What is Eckankar?" what do I say?

It's best to keep it simple. One answer could be, "It's people trying to learn more about God."

Another possibility is to say that, then ask if the other would like an Eckankar brochure. Here's where you must pay close attention. Some people are satisfied with a simple answer. Their eyes or face will say, "Oh!" They'll have just what they need.

Others want more. This second group will like your offer of an Eckankar book or brochure.

Above all, give those who ask about Eckankar no more than they want. They are who they are, what they are, and where they are—in a spiritual sense. They'd be uncomfortable if they got too much too soon.

If they want to know more about Eckankar, tell one or two things you like about it. Has it helped you? How?

A good approach, if they want to know more about Eckankar, is to tell one or two things you like about it. Has it helped you? How?

Listen to promptings from the Mahanta for guidance.

Keep it simple and light.

ECK Masters Giving Service in ECK

How do ECK Masters give service in Eckankar?

Their service is mostly quiet and unheralded. They work in the background to support the Mahanta, the Living ECK Master with his mission. The reason is that they understand that his mission is their mission. The Master's mission comes straight from the Spirit of Life, the ECK.

So how could they do otherwise?

Service in the Creative Arts

As a guitar player, I really want to go way out there and bring back the music that moves and inspires people. I also want to be unique and not copy anyone. So how can I go deeper into my music?

To play that sort of music, you need to know people. How do you do that?

Be among them; work and live as they do. Not in some idle way, as an idyllic troubadour—unless that is how you earn a living. A key phrase here is "earn a living."

Life teaches us best through our misfortunes.

Don't look for them, but do learn to take care of yourself. Divine Spirit often gives the most valuable lessons in a simple job, like dish washing. Learn to care for yourself first, for only then can you reach and serve others. That's true for a musician or anyone else.

And do the Spiritual Exercises of ECK every day.

Learn to care for yourself first, for only then can you reach and serve others.

A Door for Every Soul

I feel comfortable sharing the ECK with others, but people often ask if Eckankar is a cult. When that happens, I go within and trust the Mahanta to provide the right response. Would you please give other ways to reply to this question?

Try to find common ground with the other person. Why argue? A possible way to reply is to ask a question in return: "What do you mean by cult?" (It is a group that worships a personality. So do people who worship Jesus belong to a cult?)

Of course, most people who use the cult label want to mask their own biases. So offer something positive: an ECK book. Give them a copy of *ECKANKAR—Ancient Wisdom for Today* or *The Call of Soul*. Offer to discuss it later.

In ECK, we know the risks involved in trying to

convert others. It is against spiritual law. So if someone asks about "cult" simply to draw you into his religion, it means he doesn't know the reason for so many religions in the world.

Divine Spirit provides a door to fit every Soul.

One who tries to induce others to join his own religion is a spiritual beggar. His effort is not a sign of goodness. Rather, it shows an abuse of power, not a display of love. Avoid such people. They make loads of karma for themselves and others. Keep moving on.

Spiritual Purpose of the Temple of ECK

The Temple of ECK has been built in Chanhassen, Minnesota. Why, and what difference has it made to the whole movement of Eckankar?

I think any organization—religious, political, or social—needs a home. You need a home because you need a base to work from. But the Temple of ECK also provides a direct line of spiritual energy from the higher worlds that comes into the Physical Plane.

The Temple itself gives people an opportunity to find truth at their own level.

Now the Temple itself gives people an opportunity to find truth at their own level. The many ECK centers that are established around the world right now, and the ECK temples that will come in different parts of the world are almost like different rooms in the same Temple. It's all under the teaching of the Mahanta, the Living ECK Master—the same teacher.

It's important to have spiritual learning centers around the world for people who don't have the inner connection, yet want to get divine truth. They will have the opportunity to go to one of these ECK centers or ECK temples that will be around the world and sing HU with others and also study the spiritual discourse lessons I provide for the members of ECK.

Spiritual Golden Age

We are indeed very fortunate to live in a spiritual golden age. How can we as ECKists give greater service to all life?

The ECK teachings are for the individual. The group comes second.

A tree grows strong and tall if its character is embodied in the seed of its origin. Of greater importance, though, are other factors like soil, moisture, climate, and a favorable sun and temperature. Ideal conditions are rare. Yet add time to this recipe, then mighty oaks from acorns grow.

The point made here is from the perspective of the individual's unfoldment. The individual returns to the heart of Sugmad (God). ECK is a one-on-one path.

What behavior reveals the consciousness of a group?

Those with the eyes to see shall look for selfless deeds of love and service done without fanfare by initiates in ECK.

Such service will appear in every field of human interaction. People in religion, politics, business, and every personal endeavor that you could name will have a sure but quiet impact upon the pages of time.

Selfless deeds of love and service done without fanfare will appear in every field of human interaction.

Purpose of the Arts

What is the spiritual purpose of the arts: writing, painting, music, etc.?

This answer will come as a shock to some beginning artists and to many advanced ones as well. What is the spiritual purpose of the arts? It is to learn structure.

Until an artist has a very clear idea of how small units combine to make larger objects in God's worlds, he or she will never produce any great art.

Once an artist creates a true structure, then divine love can pour into it and make it a living thing of beauty.

Such a poem, painting, story, or piece of music helps people escape the grip of this material world and taste the joy of spiritual freedom.

Such a poem, painting, story, or piece of music by a master artist helps people escape the grip of this material world and taste the joy of spiritual freedom. So always look to see how the very smallest things around you make up bigger things.

A master artist is always a scientist first.

Can I Be Famous and Still Serve?

Is it possible to be a famous musician, actor, or even business manager, and at the same time serve the ECK in humility? Are there going to be such famous ECKists in the future? What is behind the desire to want to be famous?

Let's address your third question first.

A driving ambition to be famous for its own sake is pure vanity. It's people who think they're better than others.

But not every famous person is vain. Pure excellence in some area of knowledge or talent or inherited position that is prized in his society may have propelled him to the top. In some cases a famous person has fame set as his destiny before birth by the Lords of Karma.

Now your other two questions suggest their own answers. They fall naturally into place.

Yes, it is very possible to be a famous personality and still serve the ECK in true humility. Such an individual would always live, move, and have his being completely in ECK. He'd see himself as a servant of all living things.

And, yes, there will be such noteworthy people in ECK. It's just a matter of time.

Avoiding Conflict

When someone asks me about ECK, and they do not agree with what's being said, how can I avoid conflict and argument with that person?

This question comes up repeatedly.

There is often a clash when two sets of different beliefs bump fenders. Since no one ever really wins a heated argument, you're wise to avoid it, or leave any and all such confrontations as fast as you graciously can.

Now, that's easier said than done, isn't it?

May I suggest you read Dale Carnegie's *How to Win Friends and Influence People*? It's a fun read, full of stories. You'll like it.

Please understand that no one wants to be told he's in the wrong. But the existence of a foreign belief system nearby is like a slap in the face to some. They take offense where none is given, which is often the case with a narrow-minded person.

So you've met up with one of these classic cases. What should you do?

Such an individual would live, move, and have his being in ECK. He'd see himself as a servant of all living things.

Every situation is different, of course, but agree with him whenever or wherever it is possible. Otherwise, be still and just listen. When his steam engine runs out of fuel, all the huffing and puffing will grind to a stop.

Then say in all sincerity, "You've made some good points. They are worth thinking about. Thank you."

Excuse yourself, and leave the scene that very moment. Avoid him at all costs in the future.

Self-Discipline for a Good Leader

Part of being a good leader is allowing other people the space to serve as they can, but sometimes when people shirk their responsibilities I tend to get upset very easily.

Then I remind myself that I must not judge other people by my standards, but I also feel that self-discipline is an important part of our spiritual education. People should do what they have agreed to do. Then I seesaw between feeling upset over this issue and feeling guilty.

Could you please teach me the best way to handle this situation?

Being a good leader in a given situation starts with us. Our own self-discipline is on the line.

Being a good leader in a given situation starts with us. Our own self-discipline is on the line.

When working with a group of people, first define the task. Second, either assign the task to the most qualified person or ask for a volunteer. Third, set a deadline. Fourth, on your own calendar, set a date by which to check up on each person and ask how that person's task is coming along.

These four steps will do a lot to avoid unpleasant surprises. If someone has fallen behind, offer your help or that of another.

In this way, you remind people of the responsibility they have undertaken.

Should someone fail to finish his task by the deadline, ask what happened. Then listen. Are the reasons sound? That does beg the question, though: Why didn't you give me an update so you and I could have worked something out?

Keep a private log that lists the date, the task, the person in charge, whether it was finished on time, and last, a comments column. Do not give a task to someone who repeatedly misses a deadline.

You will thus be developing good leaders to help you tell others about the beautiful teachings of ECK.

Wondering about Giving

When people give money to those less financially well-off through a nonprofit charitable organization, are they or the organization incurring any negative karma or depriving anyone of their karmic lessons? How much does attitude play a part in avoiding the greed, power, and control issues?

Also, if someone helps a chela who can't afford the full ECK membership donation, and the chela is grateful and is contributing what he can afford, is there any negative karma incurred there?

Reputable organizations have only a small percentage of donations going to administrative costs. Their opposites, on the other hand, keep the bulk of donations for themselves. Choose your outlets for giving carefully.

Many people need help with food, shelter, and clothing. No karma is incurred if help is given in the name of the Master. Then, any giving is a spiritual act.

When people give to those less well-off, are they incurring karma or depriving anyone of their karmic lessons?

Giving anonymously or through a reputable organization does away with issues of greed, power, and control. You are out of the picture.

Nor is there any karma involved in helping a person receive the benefits of ECK membership. Turn aside offers to repay you. Encourage the individual to do the same for another when a better financial situation allows it. That makes for clean, nonkarmic giving. It is how to give in the Mahanta's name.

Back a moment to charitable organizations.

The people in a reputable group incur only good karma. Their counterparts incur the negative kind, as you would expect.

In your giving to others, it is natural to receive sincere thanks. But I would quickly, quietly, and surely distance myself from any who begin to think my gift is their due.

Inner versus Outer

You have written about the need to build a stronger "community of spirit" as we work together to bring out the ECK teachings. Is it ever OK to give an outer invitation to an inner event, such as a HU Chant, to the chela community as a whole? Can you give any guidance on how to work with the inner group consciousness?

The inner is for the inner, and the outer is for the outer.

The inner is for the inner, and the outer is for the outer.

It's OK for every chela (spiritual student) individually to invite the Mahanta into his heart. If scattered individuals heeded an area leader's suggestion to meet inwardly at a certain time for, say, a HU Chant, how long do you suppose it'd be before someone got the bright idea to direct the group's focus toward some outer project, like visualizing a temple? That'd be trying to direct the ECK. It is also a form of white magic. Don't go there.

What does "community of spirit" mean?

It refers to ECKists who live in close physical proximity to each other. Spiritual and karmic circumstances have thrown them together, so it is well for them to work together in the name of the Mahanta. They will gain spiritually by it.

Then, as an outer group, they can plan such outer projects as building an ECK temple in their area or developing a Vahana (missionary) project.

I hope this gives some clarity to the situation.

Magnets of Divine Love

I feel many future chelas (spiritual students) waiting to have you in their lives. How do we help inquirers become chelas? What is the most important thing to do? What is their process of getting from interest to inviting you into their heart?

Keep in mind that as of this very moment, all is within its rightful place in the worlds of God. This knowledge keeps us from becoming frantic.

Yet again, all within these worlds is in a continual state of flux that seeks a perfect equilibrium. It's the spiritual urge toward love and purity. But as you said, "many *future* chelas . . ."

What draws people to Eckankar?

What draws people to become members of Eckankar? Some have mentioned the appeal of being around ECKists, who are a walking testimony to the love and grace within the ECK teachings.

Others can feel a special "something" about an ECK initiate who is a living example of the divine workings of the Holy Spirit on a mundane, everyday level.

Good training can make good people much better at what they do.

But years of classroom training are unlikely to open one's heart. Others respond warmly to people with an open heart because of the love, compassion, grace, and even humor found there.

In other words, an unlettered person with an open heart is likely to be seen as an approachable source of aid, comfort, and help.

The Spiritual Exercises of ECK make us magnets of divine love.

Others see and feel the Light of God shining brightly from an ECKist who loves Sugmad (God).

That's a matter of spiritual unfoldment. It goes at its own pace, unhurried by time.

The Spiritual Exercises of ECK make us magnets of divine love. That's what draws people to us and ECK.

Regressive Therapy as a Career Path

A few years ago I became certified as a hypnotherapist. My problem is I sometimes feel hypnosis is in conflict with the ECK teachings. In a talk you said the book Journey of Souls *by Michael Newton, who does life-between-life therapy (which is the direction I'm headed), is a good read. Do I have your blessing to pursue this particular career path?*

You'll find a more complete answer to your question on pp. 25–29 of *How the Inner Master Works*, Mahanta Transcripts, Book 12, where I reply to the question Can an ECKist become a doctor who does regressive therapy?

In brief, I have no problem with it. A healing profession is a field of service, and anyone who enters it wants to do some good. Something that often goes with regressive therapy is hypnosis. As for my position on hypnotism, when it's used as a medical tool, I have no problem with that either.

Problems arise when people play with it to control others for their own purposes.

There are many different ways to use hypnotism, including mass hypnosis and other forms which I am against. On the other hand, when it is used ethically by someone in the medical profession to help heal people, to help them come to an understanding about themselves, I have no problem with it.

Regressive therapy involves hypnotizing someone to help them see past lives or remember events from their childhood. It's OK for people who are in a crisis. By all means, go to a psychotherapist if that's who you feel can give you the help you need. Psychotherapy is another way that the ECK has provided for healing.

What the patient may not realize, however, is that when the psychotherapist hypnotizes him, neither he nor the hypnotist has control over which past lives come forward on the screen of the mind.

There may be exceptions, of course, but in the case histories I've read, where someone glimpses a past life and sees incidents in which they were the victim of abuse, the person comes out of it feeling very self-righteous. Very, very seldom does psychotherapy reveal a past-life experience that makes a patient say, "The reason I was an abused child in this lifetime is because I caused it first."

I find fault with any healing method that says, "We have healed you," yet does not explain at the same time that you are responsible for your life, not someone else. The abuse you endured is the result

What the patient may not realize is neither he nor the hypnotist has control over which past lives come forward.

of the time that you once abused this person.

This does not justify their actions under the social laws. Abusers pay. But spiritual law decrees that you can only get out of life what you have put into it.

For an ECKist who is well balanced, I would suggest doing the Spiritual Exercises of ECK.

Undertake the self-discipline to learn how to go into the other worlds with the Mahanta and, with his guidance, see your past lives. This will give you a fuller understanding of the experience than hypnotherapy.

Showing Compassion

Recently I've seen my friends going through tough experiences, like a life phase of unfulfilled goals, the burden of too many duties, the injuries of a car accident, or the loss of a family member. I would love to learn more about compassion. How can I best support them?

The very worst thing one can say is "I know how you feel!"

You can't know. No one else could ever possibly know, because that person is unique. There is no one else exactly like that in thought or feeling in the whole, wide world.

How to show your compassion in the very best way? Just by listening.

How, then, to show your compassion in the very best way? Just by listening.

Really listen, without itching for the first chance to offer a solution—unless asked for one. You will learn a lot by listening, without any opinion about the other's best course of action.

You may, of course, offer words of support. If the troubled Soul, for example, was aiming and striving for a certain promotion when his company was unexpectedly bought out by another company, that position may well have gone to someone else. If appropriate, say, "You were doing all the right things. Who could have guessed?"

A grieving friend, on the other hand, may just wish to be alone. In that case, offer to run an errand or do a chore. Or bring a meal, maybe for two.

And remember to listen. That is compassion in expression. You will grow spiritually in doing so.

Choosing Your Path

It seems to me we are all doing the best we can, and that while many ECKists are not outwardly active, they may be doing other work not obvious to us.

Each chela in the ECK community is on his own individual return path to God, and it seems that accepting the trend of a group entity is an individual choice. Is my understanding accurate?

My job is to point out the smooth stretches but also the rough spots in the road to God Consciousness. Some will fix upon the rough spots.

Yesterday, in the newspaper, a columnist gave an apt description of such a person as one whose focus is on the hole in the doughnut. Others see the doughnut. Those in the second group are easy with life, for they are willing to let people be themselves. Yet this second group also knows that many beautiful Chosen People are out there, waiting to hear of the ECK teachings.

Live and let live. Each must follow his own path to God, at times in an active way and again in a quiet, restful way. You have it right.

Each must follow his own path to God, at times in an active way and again in a quiet, restful way.

Open to God's Love

*When God's
love comes
to you, it
must work
through you.*

What will help a person the most in trying to reach God-Realization? How can I open my heart more to divine love?

When God's love comes to you, it must work through you. ECKists come from all walks of life, with so many different dreams and goals, yet the spiritual thing that bonds them together is love for the Sugmad (God), the ECK, and the Mahanta.

With divine love inside them, they uplift all whom they meet. Sometimes, it's without having to say a word—like a smile to a stranger or holding a door open for someone. More often, though, this upliftment of divine love passes from an ECK Initiate through words—spoken and written—about the joy and freedom of a spiritual life.

A New Phase of Service

My perception is that we are entering a new phase in presenting the teachings of ECK to the world—a more direct approach in sharing the ECK message and the role and benefits of the Mahanta. Would you please elaborate further on your vision for presenting the Mahanta's message of love in our present time?

Your sense of this new phase is accurate. The danger to civilians from guerrilla warfare is, in some cases, reaching to shores for a long time unacquainted with this terror, like America.

This warfare upon ordinary people, the defenseless, is a political statement, of course. It is always a spiritual crime when innocent people get punished for the actions of their leaders, yet such is life. In fact, the first casualties of guerrilla warfare are so often the unarmed and helpless. Conditions like that turn a people's thoughts from self-indulgence and tranquillity to fear and uncertainty.

It is in such times that Souls begin to search for eternal values. The earthly, material ones lose their luster.

We are in a time of turmoil. People will ask, "What has real value?" "Where do we look for peace?" "Is there a way to deal with this dread and fear?"

Religion will see an awakened interest. The interest, however, will also open to nontraditional beliefs. Eckankar offers an understanding about the underlying combat always at play between good and evil. It tells the whys and wherefores of this eternal contest. And the place of love.

Karma has sped up. People will need to know the way to God's love more than ever.

Mainly, the message of love, comfort, and hope shown through the ECK teachings will be the way out of slavery from terror for many.

Karma has sped up. By 2014, the end of the 12-year cycle that began in 2002, there will be both political upheavals as well as climatic and geologic turmoil.

People will need to know the way to God's love more than ever.

Real love is selfless. We do continual acts of kindness to make the way easier for our loved ones.

11
LIVING WITH
DIVINE LOVE

Many gifts and acts of love have been given to me as a youth, especially from my parents. What are some ways that I can give this love back? In some families and societies, the parents take care of the youth, then when older, the youth take care of their parents. Should this be true to balance karmic ties, and is this true at all?

You have a good way of looking at the give-and-take of love.

Love shows itself in deeds of love. People who love people are the luckiest people in the world.

Real love is selfless. We do continual acts of kindness to make the way easier for our loved ones.

By giving love, we become magnets of love.

The happiest people I know are those who give and receive love from their families and friends. Now, we're talking about the "no-strings-attached" kind of love. We do chores around the home with cheerfulness. Of course, we have bad days. But love tries to keep those days in check.

Love shows itself in deeds of love.

How would you want others to treat you? Treat them the same way.

Spiritually healthy people like to be a ray of sunshine for the ones they love. So too will children, when grown, do what they can to ease the trials of aging for their parents. Little things count.

Count all the little everyday things your parents did for you as a child. Someday they'll need someone to do the same for them.

Yes, some families and societies have the practice of mutual care between parents and children at the different stages of life. Most people do so under the Law of Karma. That is just and right.

An ECKist, a member of Eckankar, though, acts in accord with a higher law, the Law of Love. It allows more joy and freedom for all members of the family.

The Spiritual Quest

What is the spiritual quest?

The spiritual quest is to live a God-Realized life.

What's at the core of God-Realization if not divine love? So, the quest means learning to give and receive God's love in an always-increasing measure. One doesn't have to run around frantically in search of it. Sugmad's love is all around.

Divine love is always with you. But you must open your heart to it.

Like the Mahanta, divine love is always with you. But you must learn to open your heart to it.

One way is by doing an easy spiritual exercise, which I'll give you here.

The key is to contemplate on all the things in your life that you're grateful for, like your family and friends, your health, your opportunities, or the Mahanta.

Then sit or lie down and get comfortable. Next, begin to sing "Thank you," either aloud or silently. Let a parade of all the things you're grateful for march across the screen of your mind, from left to right. This is a pleasant exercise. It will begin to open your heart to Sugmad in a greater way than ever before.

The quest! People have pursued it across the pages of history, yet it has always eluded them. They were looking for a precious treasure out there. But it was hidden in their very own hearts the whole time.

People were looking for a treasure out there. But it was hidden in their very own hearts.

In Face of Change

Life brings many changes. How can I embrace every new opportunity with an open heart? How can I keep the heart awakened, alive, listening, surrendered at each moment, and filled with gratitude? And what golden ethics do I always need to keep in my heart as an ECKist?

You make a good connection in that some people instinctively shut down their openness when the wind of change comes through the window. The mind is like a mule. It knows what it knows, has full confidence in the poverty of its capacity, and has even built an iron box to safely store the whole of what it knows. That box, to the mind, is security.

The wind of change is mightier than might first appear. Our mind cannot resist it. So a lock on the iron box mysteriously opens, and the top swings up. Change comes in.

So what makes the heart and mind close if not fear?

Fear is indeed the bogeyman. And what does

that suggest other than a lack of trust that the ECK is doing everything for our spiritual good. All I can suggest to counter fear is to love God and others more. And ask the Mahanta to open your heart again.

That is the answer to your first two concerns.

As to ethics: Would you be proud if the Mahanta, the Living ECK Master saw you conduct your affairs?

Open the Heart

How can I open my heart to love?

Have you heard of the spiritual exercise that one writes fifteen times each day? It's an open invitation to the ECK to bring a certain desire into manifestation. It will bring a series of changes, small and subtle at first because you need time to absorb them. The spiritual desire to write fifteen times each day is this: "I am love." That's it.

The spiritual desire to write fifteen times each day is "I am love."

At your discretion you may add or subtract other spiritual desires like wisdom, understanding, life, joy, health, wealth (yes, it's OK to ask), and whatever else that the Inner Master prompts you to ask for. Then stand back and watch the ECK bring changes into your life. If It wants to.

Deeper Meaning of HU Chants

What is the deeper meaning behind the HU chant?

It's something I can't tell you out here. What is revealed to an individual about the secret name of God depends on the readiness of the person's heart.

The chanting of the HU in groups is very important. It binds our spiritual community together. It creates a purifying wave and carries away a lot of the petty things that an organization in an area might get into. There's a great deal of purification that goes on at HU Chants.

But the more arcane mysteries of the HU chant are revealed as a person is ready and really more than that I can't say. Because the mysteries don't mean anything out here. Usually the meaning is for no one else but you. It's very personal.

Sometimes what you'll find as the inner doors to the name of HU are opened are different ways to chant. You are given a different key, a different way to reach further into the inner worlds. It depends upon you. But there are many dimensions to what the HU chant does to open you in this direction.

Enlightened Soul

In We Come as Eagles, *Mahanta Transcripts, Book 9, you write that an eagle is a symbol of the enlightened Soul. One day, I saw at least a hundred eagles circling the sky. It was a sight to behold. What is the spiritual symbolism of this experience?*

The eagle is a symbol of spiritual principles, of Divine Spirit. It is a symbol of great significance to you.

To see a hundred eagles is a spiritual blessing, for it is the Mahanta's way of saying that you can reach new heights in your quest for God's love. But several things are needed.

The eagle speaks of nobility, yet it requires one to put aside a fear of the unknown. In addition, it means the ability to accept all experiences in life, the good and the bad, and realize that they are to help you receive more divine love. You must also learn to look

All experiences in life, the good and the bad, are to help you receive more divine love.

for opportunities beyond your present horizon.

Read more about the eagle in Paul Twitchell's *The ECK-Vidya, Ancient Science of Prophecy.*

Living Love

How can love be with me? This question is difficult for me because sometimes I feel sad. Happiness just seems to run out, and happiness is love.

Thank you for a very good question.

First, happiness isn't necessarily love. It's one of the things that comes from love. The Mahanta's love is always with you. That means he's with you in both happy and sad times, looking out for your best spiritual good.

Soul (you) is here to learn how to become more like God's pure qualities of love.

Second, God is love, but not everything here is love. Remember, earth is a school. Soul (you) is here to learn how to become more like God's pure qualities of love. We learn most from our troubles, not always from the good times.

It helps to know this world for what it is—good and evil. The Mahanta's love helps you avoid many of the hard times and find the good.

There is only one of you in this world. But there are always a few people who think and feel as you do. Open your heart to them. Be their friend. Ignore the ones who are not like you.

The secret is this: You make your own happiness. And that begins with the company you keep.

Learning a Spiritual Skill

I'm a fourteen-year-old ECKist. Even though I do my spiritual exercises regularly, I'm not having any experiences, like a dream or even just seeing a blue light. Can you please help me to have an experience? Also, my dad says he sees the ECK in everything. What does he mean?

May I encourage you to keep on with the Spiritual Exercises of ECK!

Remember how long it took to learn the skill of writing? Now you can dash off the alphabet without a second thought, as well as string combinations of letters together to form words and sentences.

The pattern of learning a spiritual skill requires much the same diligence. For a long time there may appear to be no progress at all, yet a foundation is in the making. By no means become frantic. The Mahanta waits until an individual gains a solid spiritual footing. Then he opens the Spiritual Eye.

That's what your dad is trying to explain when he says he sees the ECK (Divine Spirit) in everything.

The Master has opened his Spiritual Eye.

ECK has a thousand faces. Some see Its presence as some color of light, in dozens of possible shapes. Others, like your dad, see Its workings in everyday people, places, and situations.

ECK likewise has a thousand voices. Some hear It speak through any of dozens of possible voices: storms, birds, laughter, falling or moving water, rushing air, and even in the sounds of machinery.

Some perceive both the Light and Sound of God. Give it time.

ECK has a thousand faces. Likewise a thousand voices.

State of Consciousness and Initiation Level

How much difference, if any, does the initiation level and state of consciousness of a person make to the growth and unfoldment of an area? Is it a matter of how much love the person can share or hold?

A person's state of consciousness matters a great deal; his initiation level does not.

And it is as you suggest: love determines the growth and unfoldment of an area. It's all about God's love. Everything begins and ends with divine love in the worlds of creation. So, necessarily, that applies many times over when it comes to the level of consciousness in an area.

People can sense who you are at heart.

For this reason, fill your heart with love and let your contemplation be: "Not my will, but Thine, be done." Then go about your duties with a light and cheerful heart.

Keys to God-Realization

In Soul Travelers of the Far Country, *you write:
"I once asked the Inner Master, 'Are love and compassion the keys to God-Realization?' He said no, then fell silent."*

What are the keys to God-Realization? And do these keys change as our consciousness expands?

You ask the same good question now as I did then. Paul Twitchell had once remarked that the Master may make a statement, then fall silent. The reason is to pique the deepest sort of interest in the questioner.

Paul knew that anything of real value must come through effort—the more the better. Otherwise that gem of wisdom would likely be glanced at casually, tossed aside, and the questions would start all over again. So, rather than leave you without a clue at all, I'll expand on this question.

The key (note the singular) to God-Realization is love, and love alone.

All else comes from love. So my question was of a two-pronged assumption that love *and* compassion, *two* keys, were the secret to God-Realization. The Inner Master, by strict definition, but without expanding on his answer, simply said, "No."

He meant that love and love alone is the key to God-Realization. All other attributes and virtues spring from divine love. It is the beginning and ending of all things.

Love is the key to God-Realization.

Does Soul's understanding—rather Its realization—of love as the key change as Its consciousness expands?

Yes.

Benefits of HU

What does the HU do?

It opens your heart to the Sugmad, the ECK (Holy Spirit), and the Mahanta. In other words, HU opens you to God's sweet love.

HU opens you to God's sweet love.

Guidance of the Divine Presence

The principle of doing everything in the name of the Sugmad (God), the ECK, or the Mahanta is central to Eckankar and to the training and discipline of every Soul in Its quest for God-Realization. Could you please expand a little on what it means to act "in the name of" the Sugmad or the Mahanta?

It is very easy to do.

First, declare yourself an open channel. You may

do it on this order: "I declare myself a vehicle for the Sugmad, the ECK, and the Mahanta." Then go about your business.

Making such a declaration lifts you into a new frame of awareness, a more heightened state of consciousness.

You will become aware of the Divine Presence as It guides you past situations that would normally vex you or cause trepidation.

This technique is especially helpful when you must venture into some dark or uncertain stream in your life, a crossroads or a crisis. You will become acutely aware of the Divine Presence as It guides you past situations that would normally vex you or cause trepidation.

Picture yourself as a child of God.

You will then find the courage to step boldly into the unknown and confront yourself.

Mercy

You refer to the Ocean of Love and Mercy when speaking about Sugmad (God). You have made great efforts to give us a feel for divine love. I don't recall, however, anything said or written about divine mercy or compassion of any kind. Would you please discuss mercy and how it fits in with your mission?

Mercy and compassion are two very important qualities, but love is the greatest of all.

From top to bottom, Sugmad is the Ocean of Love and Mercy. "Life has no existence," says *The Shariyat*, Book One, "but for the love and mercy of God." Yet one can only find the Mahanta, the Living ECK Master if he has love and humility and shows compassion (mercy) toward others.

"Love is the passkey to the kingdom of heaven," says *The Shariyat*, Book Two.

To date, the focus in ECK has been on divine love. There is a reason for that. So many people, inside and outside of ECK, have the upside-down notion that mercy is a divine quality that God and others owe them. Such thinking is part of the push for "entitlements" that has gained favor in society since the founding of Eckankar in the mid-1960s. The imprint of this attitude upon the minds of Western society is spelled out in an old prayer: "Lord, have mercy upon me, a poor sinful being."

Such a view of mercy puts out the creative spark in Soul. It makes for passive people.

In ECK, we go in steps. Love and mercy are equally important in the ECK doctrines. Yet our attention so far has been upon divine love because of what mercy implies: a position of strength from which to show compassion for the less fortunate. An ECK Master, for example, speaks from a position of spiritual strength. Thus, mercy from him can do miracles, like opening the gates of heaven for an individual with a mere glance. Yet mercy from a slave counts for little, because he has so little control over his own destiny.

The second of the four Zoas (laws for Higher Initiates in Eckankar) lists compassion among the qualities of the Mahdis (Higher Initiate). It does so with the understanding that all who reach the Atma Lok (Soul Plane) know their mission: to become a Co-worker with God. That role means giving love and mercy to all.

Further, the Spiritual Exercises of ECK impart wisdom. They give an insight on how compassion shrinks the walls between Souls, for how could anyone not have compassion for another Light of God in need of a smile, a kind word, or even a meal?

To become a Co-worker with God means giving love and mercy to all.

Euthanasia

Would you like to talk about euthanasia?

This subject brings up a lot of heated debate, both pro and con. If it were ever to become a part of government policy, that would be a major spiritual crime. The sick and the elderly would get poor treatment under government-sponsored health plans simply because of the cost. It would lead to government-sanctioned murder.

On the other end of the scale, on the individual's end, I point out the spiritual principle of being a survivor under any condition, if possible.

Yet if someone commits suicide, who is to know how much that person was suffering? At any rate, it is best to withhold your judgment. You don't want to put yourself in those same shoes. Cause and effect, you know.

Assisted Suicide

On a spiritual and moral level, what is Eckankar's viewpoint of assisted suicide?

The teachings of ECK, I hope, will awaken the survival factor in all of you. So no matter what happens, whatever comes, you will show a can-do spirit. You know that somehow there's a way. And as long as there is life, you will do everything in your power to keep on living.

The point is, if you can't survive here, how do you expect to survive in the other worlds?

Both will present even stiffer challenges if you take the "easy" way out. So meet yourself here and now. Unless you do, you're going to meet yourself some other place. And when you look in a mirror,

The teachings of ECK, I hope, will awaken the survival factor in all of you.

you'll never know yourself because of new skin and a mind washed clean of things past.

Sometimes people criticize those who do commit suicide. My stand on it is to see life through to its natural end. But if the pain ever becomes so great, and you ask the doctor to please help you be free of this life, I will never say a word. Who am I to speak, unless I have walked in your shoes?

That decision is yours, not mine.

Expect, but Accept

As I was walking the corridors of a hospital recently, I came upon a woman who had just lost a loved one. For a fraction of a second I felt all her sorrow and pain. For a moment, we were one. I was surprised. Later I realized it was true compassion. I have tried to give compassion to situations since then when there is someone in need, but that higher level never came back again. How could I learn to give more love and compassion?

Nothing is ever the same as it was.

If life has a single lesson to teach us, it's that. Many lessons and experiences are similar, but no two will ever be exactly alike. The best approach to spiritual unfoldment is to expect the greatest love and blessings from the divine ECK, but then accept whatever comes your way.

Expect, but accept.

The ECK will always take you, in time, beyond your wildest dreams. But then you've got to be ready to accept them. No matter what. Nothing is ever lost in God's creation, because all experiences lead Soul to the higher path of love and compassion.

Expect the greatest love and blessings from the divine ECK, but then accept whatever comes your way.

Obedience

I have been noticing references in The Shariyat-Ki-Sugmad *to obedience. Could you comment on the role of this quality in Eckankar, which embraces spiritual freedom?*

True spiritual freedom comes through a complete and loving obedience to the divine trinity of the Sugmad, ECK, and the Mahanta, the Living ECK Master. Obedience and surrender of the little self to the divine will go hand in hand. A chela (spiritual student of ECK) listens for the Holy Word and obeys It. And, of course, the divine will works directly through the Mahanta, so how could a true seeker of God do other than to obey the Master? The Mahanta, the Living ECK Master asks only that of a chela which is in the latter's spiritual interest.

As an aside, speaking of benefits on the path of ECK, there is a significant one that occurs at the time of translation.

If one whispers the name of the Mahanta at the moment of death, he will never have to return to this physical universe again. He is immediately taken into the spiritual worlds for a more complete freedom. And if unconscious at the time of passing from the human body, another chela may quietly repeat the Master's name with the same effect at the side of the unconscious one.

And a final word of encouragement: Read again "The Circles of ECK Initiations" given in *The Shariyat-Ki-Sugmad*, Book Two. It will help to keep your vision upon the goal of God Consciousness.

The Mahanta, the Living ECK Master asks only that of a chela which is in the latter's spiritual interest.

What Happens after Death?

What happens to us after death?

I'll paint a picture of the afterlife with a broad brush. The reason is that consciousness is like a river of water in that it goes gradually from a small stream to a larger one.

A composer, for example, uses a similar method. When he wishes to move up, say, eleven notes from a starting note, he will work his way up in gradual steps rather than in one big leap. He may go up two notes, drop back a half note, move up a full note, and so on, until he reaches the eleventh note he was aiming for.

These gradual movements from the smaller to the larger or the lower to the higher are to prevent a destructive or jarring effect upon the sensibilities of man or nature.

So it is, too, when an individual moves from this life to the afterlife. It is within the limits of one's expectations.

Of course, we do not speak here about the particular event that causes death, such as an accident, other violence, or even a peaceful passing in bed after reaching a ripe old age. Our attention is upon what sort of life one can expect in the other worlds after his passing.

It will be similar to what an individual gains on earth and his spiritual state of consciousness. If he embraces the images and conditions of a Christian, he will start there in the continuation of his life in the other worlds.

Soul must use the earthly life to expand in consciousness via the Spiritual Exercises of ECK.

These exercises open a person's heart to God's

When an individual moves from this life to the afterlife, it is within the limits of one's expectations.

love, which is to help and comfort all. With this understanding, one may then become a real spiritual traveler. He begins his mission as a Co-worker with God. Everything is an open book. Life is a joyful, interesting, and useful one, of service to all.

Any number of ECK Masters can appear over the span of one's lifetime to help ease the way.

12
ECK MASTERS AND THE WORLDS OF GOD

Are the ECK Masters, the Order of the Vairagi Adepts, archetypal images or real beings?

These are real beings. There are people who have had experiences with Rebazar Tarzs years before they knew about the ECK Masters or became members of Eckankar. Or they've had experiences with Yaubl Sacabi and Fubbi Quantz. These ECK Masters served at the height of civilization throughout our history.

The ECK Masters have great compassion. They give love and mercy to the people they meet. All they want to do is pass along the gifts of God, but people have to earn them.

There are always the spiritually advanced among mankind.

Earliest Masters on Earth

How did the first beings become ECK Masters when the consciousness was at such a low level?

First, there are always the spiritually advanced

among mankind. It has been so from earth's earliest times. Those early candidates for ECK Mastership chose to come to earth in those days out of their great love for struggling Souls. Their own connection was with ECK Masters on the upper planes. As above, so below. This principle was at work then even as it is now.

Those early candidates were under the guidance of Masters like Malati.

Second, some of these ECK Masters had gained their Mastership before descending to earth. They willingly accepted human birth as a means of spiritual service to early races.

Roots of Eckankar

In ancient times the Living ECK Master gave the ECK teachings by word of mouth.

Where or in what country did Eckankar begin?

In ancient times, the Living ECK Master gave the ECK teachings to his disciples by word of mouth. Rama was among the first of these Masters. *The Shariyat-Ki-Sugmad* says he came from the forests of northern Germany.

From there, he traveled to Iran (ancient Persia), where he gave the secret teachings to a small band of mystics. Their descendants were later to become the followers of Zoroaster, around 600 BC. But the first ECK writings did not appear until much later, around the thirteenth century. Rumi, the Persian poet, was about the first writer to hint at them, which he did in his famous poem "The Reed of God."

After leaving Persia, Rama moved to India, where he settled down. *The Shariyat* says he taught people there about the chance to have the experience of God in that very lifetime.

So where did Eckankar begin?

Even before Rama, the ECK teachings were in Atlantis and Lemuria. Modern scholars scoff at the existence of those two lost continents, so we don't talk much about them in Eckankar today. Yet proof does exist. Under the waters off the southeastern part of the United States are huge stone blocks in the shape of a wall or an ancient road. Somebody put them there a long time ago, when that part of the ocean was above water.

ECK Masters around the World

Are there any ECK Masters from West Africa? If so, what are their names?

ECK Masters work in all parts of the world today. Few stay in a single geographical region for long.

In any age, the chief agent for the Sugmad is the Mahanta, the Living ECK Master. In whatever century and country he lives, he serves every Soul, regardless of race or creed. His only purpose is to help people find spiritual freedom.

Of course, the Mahanta cannot help those who resist truth.

A Master, even from one's own race, is of no help unless the individual is spiritually ready for him. For example, a friend from his boyhood town may find it especially hard to accept him. The mind likes to chew over unimportant details as an excuse to reject him.

If someone fails to move ahead spiritually with the Mahanta, the Living ECK Master, chances are he won't be much better off with an ECK Master from his own country.

Do you still want to meet an ECK Master? It takes a strong desire. If you have it, one will come

ECK Masters work in all parts of the world today.

whether your home is in West Africa, Hong Kong, or South America. He will find you.

Golden Wisdom Temples

In ECK Wisdom Temples, Spiritual Cities, & Guides: A Brief History *it says: "House of Moksha . . . ECK Master Rami Nuri is guardian of the Shariyat here." And "Temple of ECK, Sri Harold Klemp, the Mahanta, the Living ECK Master is guardian of this temple." Could you explain the difference between a guardian of the Shariyat and a guardian of the temple?*

They're the same.

The descriptions in *The Shariyat-Ki-Sugmad* of the Golden Wisdom Temples and their management is sketchy. In many cases, it sounds as if it's a one-man show.

However, the ECK Master in charge is like a chief executive officer (CEO) of a modern organization. He runs an entire staff. It includes the assistance of other ECK Masters who help him with the normal duties one would expect in a spiritual and administrative center.

Some ECK Masters at a Temple of Golden Wisdom serve in more than one capacity.

Some ECK Masters at a Temple of Golden Wisdom serve in more than one capacity. For example, a keeper of records may double as an Arahata (teacher), while a master gardener is equally adept as one who specializes in teaching a course in spiritual ethics.

There are also other initiates on staff who carry out things that need doing. Yes, someone even cleans the floors. Another initiate is an expert at inventory control. And there are receptionists and secretaries, and those who prepare food.

Some who hear of these daily workings may

think such duties are unspiritual. Be that as it may.

But remember that earth is a reflection of what is above. So look around. The interests and pursuits of things around us have a model on the higher planes.

I hope this gives you a better understanding of how the Temples of Golden Wisdom, here and there, operate as an expression of love for Sugmad.

It's a very matter-of-fact universe.

Blessing of Service to God

What's it like being the Mahanta, the Living ECK Master?

First, it's a blessing and privilege beyond all understanding. It's a gift from Sugmad (God). God appoints the one who stands as the divine emissary, and so the latter's loyalty is bound by love in eternity.

Second, this position is all about having the doors of learning life's big and little secrets thrown wide open.

Some think the Mahanta, the Living ECK Master has all human and divine knowledge in the palm of his hand. In a spiritual sense, yes.

However, the human mind is but a thimble dipping water from a river. The water collected is as little as what the mind can catch and hold of the full magnitude and glory of spiritual things.

Yet a thimbleful of water can capture the quality and nature of the whole river. It's all contained in a single drop.

Third, the hearts of people are an open book. The Master sees and knows the thinking and feelings behind people's behavior. Yes, he sees the envy, ambition, and greed. But those negative mental traits

This position is all about having the doors of learning life's big and little secrets thrown wide open.

are in all of the human consciousness, so people's shames are all on the table before him.

Yet the Master sees the light of Soul in each person. It's the part in mankind that yearns for God. That's what he loves.

The Shariyat-Ki-Sugmad, Book One, gives a whole chapter on who and what I see and know. Read chapter 6, "The Living ECK Master." You'll get a look at what it's like on the Master's side of the curtain of life. There are some astounding facts about him, and more chelas (spiritual students) would help themselves in a spiritual way if they read chapter 6 too.

Gratitude for Training

Do your parents know that you are a top ECK Master?

My father translated (died) a month after Paul Twitchell's translation on September 17, 1971. My dad's job of training me was finished. Many, often including myself, would have found him to be a most difficult and demanding teacher.

In 2005, my mother translated. She was a devout Christian and said her prayers before meals and at bedtime.

She was comfortable with Jesus Christ as her Lord. And though she knew in a general way that I have the good fortune to be the leader of Eckankar, she didn't understand the spiritual importance of that. I wrote a letter to her every week. The letter was about everyday matters like cooking, her grandchildren and great grandchildren. I tried to lift her spirits.

My parents gave my brothers, sister, and me much love despite the often severe conditions on a Midwest dairy farm.

I have much gratitude for their role in my spiritual development.

Peddar Zaskq

Is Paul Twitchell in charge of a Golden Wisdom Temple on the inner planes? If so, which one? And if not, what is he doing?

At present, Peddar Zaskq (the spiritual name of Paul Twitchell) is not in charge of a Temple of Golden Wisdom. Like Rebazar Tarzs, he moves from place to place as an agent for Sugmad. He goes to those in need of spiritual aid.

Every so often we touch base. Like all the ECK Masters, the many duties in his care fill the day.

Like my dad, Peddar Zaskq gave me an abundance of both love and discipline. The outer and inner tests and trials were such that I was often at a loss to know where to find the spiritual strength to meet them.

ECK Masters, like Peddar, are like cousins or, better, brothers to me. They and I know and respect each other's missions. We work in full agreement.

Peddar Zaskq moves from place to place as an agent for Sugmad (God). He goes to those in need of spiritual aid.

Other Brotherhoods

Is the Vairagi Order, of which you are the present leader, connected to any other brotherhood? And if not, do you still work with other masters and teachers?

It's an independent spiritual order. But we work with the masters of the other orders because among the true leaders of any spiritual teaching—where people are truly interested in the spiritual welfare of the human race—there aren't any walls.

Each of these groups of spiritual adepts knows that it has a particular function to carry out. Each group has its own mission to God. There is no conflict. They allow people to go to whichever group they need to for their own spiritual unfoldment.

Wah Z

What is your spiritual name, and what is the meaning of a spiritual name?

Wah Z is my spiritual name. It is the whole name. Sometimes people on the inner planes call me "Z" for short. But it's all my name.

The name of an ECK Master has a spiritual power to it. Whispering or singing "Wah Z" softly before bedtime may help you meet me in your dreamlands. Our meetings there can bring you peace and rest through the night. And some interesting adventures.

Some ECK Masters do have spiritual names that act like first and last names. Take Rebazar Tarzs. Sometimes people call him Rebazar for short. But his spiritual name is Rebazar Tarzs.

Other names are simpler, being only one word, so there's no question about first or last name. Some that come to mind are Milarepa, Agnotti, Castrog, Gakko, Rama, Malati, and more.

Lai Tsi's name has two syllables. Yet he is always addressed as Lai Tsi—no first or last name either.

Whispering or singing "Wah Z" softly before bedtime may help you meet me in your dreamlands.

Working with the ECK Masters

I have a strong affinity with one of the other ECK Masters who has helped me many times on the inner. I am thankful for this, but sometimes I get confused

*about whom I should place my attention on. Should
it be the Mahanta, the Living ECK Master or this
other ECK Master?*

True ECK Masters work in harmony with the
Mahanta, the Living ECK Master. The reason is
simple, for they are the ECK.

The Mahanta, the Living ECK Master often
assigns a certain ECK Master to work with an ECK
chela (spiritual student) during a certain phase of
the chela's inner unfoldment. The ECK Master is a
mentor.

Any number of ECK Masters can appear over
the span of one's lifetime to help ease the way.
Accept the blessing of each ECK Master's presence.
You'll be the better for it.

*True ECK
Masters work
in harmony
with the
Mahanta,
the Living
ECK Master.*

Soul's Unselfish Giving

*I know Santa Claus doesn't come down our
chimney on Christmas Eve, but in my mind he does
exist. Was he ever real, and is he an ECK Master?*

The tradition of Santa Claus dates back to fourth-
century Turkey. St. Nicholas was a bishop there.
Many legends exist about St. Nicholas, the name-
sake for Santa Claus, but today there is little real
information about his life or his deeds.

After the death of St. Nicholas, many people
adopted him as a patron saint, especially in Russia.
That was long before the rise of Communism there
in the early twentieth century. But the Protestant
Reformation made reverence for saints less popular
throughout the countries of Europe. So St. Nicholas
fell out of favor there.

In Holland, though, the people continued to give

respect to St. Nicholas, whom they called Sinterklaas.

When the Dutch immigrated to what is now New York in the seventeenth century, they brought the tradition of Sinterklaas with them. He was not connected with Christmas, though.

English settlers in New York liked the idea of Sinterklaas, but they changed his name to Santa Claus. (Say "Sinterklaas" fast and it's hard to tell it apart from "Santa Claus.")

Whether Sinterklaas or Santa Claus, the mission is the same. It is to bring gifts to children.

So the tradition encourages giving.

Whatever name this spirit of giving thrives under, it is certainly a virtue. Both Sinterklaas and Santa Claus are ideal role models. They show that the nature of Soul is to give unselfishly of Itself to others.

I Am Always with You

If I ask for you as the Mahanta to be with me, how do I know you are really there or if it is just me pretending you are there?

A skeptic would say there's no way to know.

And so might some people who've been in Eckankar since babyhood, since they grew up with the presence of the Mahanta and have come to take it for granted.

Pay more attention to your dreams, spiritual exercises, and the little "coincidences" that gently flow in and out of your life.

If all is pretty nearly going well for you, pay more attention to your dreams, your spiritual exercises, and the little "coincidences" that gently flow in and out of your life. Not just to the ones that turn out in your favor. But look also for the moments when a little thing seems to go wrong for you—yet teaches or reminds you of what is right or wrong.

Those little incidents will be examples of the Mahanta's presence. There is also a spiritual principle that you are already doing: "Act as if." For example, if you want the Mahanta in your life as a spiritual guide, act as if he is.

He is anyway, of course, but it will help you to stay aware of his presence.

Now, this is earth, a school for Soul's spiritual education. It is much better at teaching people than any public or private school. The lessons and tests of spiritual living will crop up around you at any and all times, unsuspected as such.

Sometimes it will be the Kal, the negative force, whispering through your closest friend, "Ah, smoke it. One puff won't hurt."

That's a test. To pass it, remember to act "as if" and ask, "What should I do, Mahanta?" Guess. Friends once said that to me. I said, "I don't need it."

Keep your eyes and heart open. I *am* always with you.

Soul's Choice

Why can't a female be the Mahanta, the Living ECK Master?

The Sugmad (God) appoints the male who is to be the next Mahanta, the Living ECK Master. It is always a male.

Why?

A Soul in training for the role of the Mahanta, the Living ECK Master enters this life as a male. Women can and do become ECK Masters, as you know. The reason for this choice of a male for the position of the Mahanta, the Living ECK Master is a spiritual one.

The Living ECK Master enters this life as a male. Women can and do become ECK Masters.

Look in *The Shariyat-Ki-Sugmad*, Book Two, in the middle of chapter 7, for the answer.

It explains: "The male is positive, active, and progressive, while the female is passive, reactive, or responsive as it may seem to the observer, and retrogressive."

In the next paragraph, it explains further. It says, "There is no such thing as a total male type in this world, nor could there be a total female type either. Since man and woman are living in a negative, or passive, world of matter, all concerned have a certain amount of the negative within them, merely to keep those living in the physical body alive, to adapt to the needs of existence."

Every Living ECK Master goes through the initiation of accepting the Rod of ECK Power. It is then that he accepts the spiritual mantle.

During this initiation the ECK descends and enters into him. It imparts the power of the Word of God.

Yes, today some find it hard to accept these pure ECK teachings. It is because of egotism. So they dispute these words of the Master and become snide with him. They never understand the troubles that befall them as a result.

By doing the exercises, an individual says, "Please help me work out my karma and find God."

Why Spiritual Exercises?

Do you ever get really frustrated with ECKists who don't do their spiritual exercises? I know you are the Master, but you are also human, so does that ever affect you?

I let all Souls go at their own pace. Yes, it is clear when an individual is making problems by forgetting to do the ECK Spiritual Exercises. It's part of learning.

The spiritual exercises are a good habit, like a student remembering to lock valuables in a school locker. It avoids trouble.

The practice of the exercises forms a pact with the Master. By doing them, an individual says, "Please help me work out my karma and find God." Then the Master lets unnecessary karma burn off without the chela (spiritual student) having to live through it.

It makes life more pleasant and meaningful.

So you see, there is a real advantage for chelas who do their spiritual exercises.

Roles of Living ECK Master

You are the Living ECK Master of Eckankar, and you also embody the Mahanta Consciousness. Could you explain these two roles?

People talk about the Mahanta Consciousness as being something that you slip on and off like a shirt. But, in fact, the person who takes on the role of spiritual leader and has a certain level of spiritual growth then becomes both the Mahanta and the Living ECK Master; which means the Mahanta is the inner side of the teacher and the Living ECK Master is the outer side of the teacher.

The Mahanta is the inner side of the teacher and the Living ECK Master is the outer side of the teacher.

This gives a balance of both the inner and outer teachings so that the individual can have a clear, unobstructed path back home to God.

Mahanta Consciousness

Do you shift in and out of the Mahanta Consciousness? And if you do, are you aware of when you are working from there or not?

I am aware of the ECK in, around, and through me always. There is never a moment that I am not aware of Its love and presence.

It envelops my being. I am aware of that every minute and am truly grateful to It for the gift of life. The ECK is my heartbeat. It abides in me, flows through me, giving Its blessings to all, whether or not they accept or believe It. It lets me see the goodness in people, though it often hides far beneath the surface.

ECK is life; It is love. That's why I try to show others their own way to It.

Mahanta 24/7

You have often stated that the Mahanta Consciousness operates within the Living ECK Master twenty-four hours a day. What sort of adjustments do you have to make to be able to work with the Mahanta Consciousness all the time?

Please understand, the Mahanta, the Living ECK Master is the ECK Itself. He is by nature the holy Life Stream. The Divine Current has no on-off spigot. Therefore, the divine wisdom is his every living moment.

Paul Twitchell, for example, had someone run a tape recorder when his words were especially meant for truth seekers. This was when he was with a secretary, ECK leaders, at a public talk, or in an interview. But he remained in that full state of consciousness also when having a cup of tea with Gail, his wife.

He was in it, too, down at the coffee shop. Paul was fully conscious of the holy Life Current all the time, day and night.

Do you see? The Master's state of consciousness is unlike anyone else's.

There is no need to make midcourse adjustments in that regard.

Vision of the Mahanta

I often hear ECK leaders refer to the Mahanta's vision. What is the Mahanta's vision?

The Mahanta's vision is to reach all Souls who are ready with the teachings of ECK.

Living ECK Master and Mahanta

I've heard that the next Living ECK Master may not be the Mahanta. How is this possible?

The answer to your question is given in full in the ECK writings. May I direct you to *Wisdom of the Heart*, Book 2, Letter 37: "The Living ECK Master and the Mahanta, the Living ECK Master."

This chapter recalls words from *The Shariyat-Ki-Sugmad*, Book Two. The small details are too fine to go into here.

Conscious-ness is an individual matter. So each Master is at a unique point in spiritual evolution.

But, in short, consciousness is an individual matter. So each Master is at a unique point in spiritual evolution when he accepts the Rod of ECK Power. A majority are ECK initiates of the Twelfth Circle. They are the Maharaji.

On the other hand, the Mahanta, the Living ECK Master is an ECK initiate of the Fourteenth Circle. He is a Mahanta.

A key to the difference between a Maharaji and a Mahanta, says *The Shariyat*, is that "the Maharaji lives only in the body and does not have the spiritual power which the Mahanta does, for the latter *inherits* [italics added] the ECK Rod of Power and the Maharaji is only *appointed* [italics added] to his position."

And yet the Maharaji carries the spiritual title of Mahanta. It is a sign of respect for the spiritual position.

There are many fine points in that Wisdom Note, Letter 37.

Read with an open heart. If you do, the window of understanding will reveal the answer to even your unspoken questions.

For more on the ECK Masters, look in both books of *Wisdom of the Heart*. The chapter headings give a quick reference to the workings and nature of the ECK Masters. Read with an open heart. If you do, the window of understanding will reveal the answer to even your unspoken questions.

Levels of Mahanta Consciousness

Sometime in the future will the Living ECK Master not hold the Mahanta Consciousness? And will the next Living ECK Master care as much about the children, youth, and young adults—the future of Eckankar—as you do?

Let me again explain about the Living ECK Masters. One of the Fourteenth Circle *is* a Mahanta. One of the Twelfth or Thirteenth Circle is of the Mahanta Consciousness.

What is the difference?

The full might and glory passes through a full Mahanta, while a lesser amount, to some degree or other, passes through one of the Mahanta Consciousness. One of the past ECK Masters was the equivalent of a Fifth Initiate today. He was the most highly advanced ECK initiate of that time.

For all that, a Living ECK Master of the Mahanta

Consciousness is to be accorded the full respect and honor of the Master. His proper title, according to *The Shariyat-Ki-Sugmad*, is the Mahanta, the Living ECK Master.

Please know that he'll care as much about the ECK children, youth, and young adults as I do.

A side note: Every Living ECK Master remains until his mission is complete. His successor has finished his training when his Master steps aside.

Spiritual Timing

On October 22, 1996, while I was at work, I seemed to notice a subtle shift in space, time, or consciousness (I don't know how else to describe it). Looking back on it later, I saw on the inner planes a round clocklike structure with two or three beings standing in front of it, as if they had adjusted it. What was occurring?

The subtle shift you felt on the ECK New Year of 1996 was indeed that of space, time, and consciousness. It means of both your own universe and also the larger ECK theater.

There were three ECK Masters. They adjust the spiritual timing of when and how the ECK teachings are to be at the best position for the ever-evolving consciousness of people. The clock is a sort of regulator. These ECK Masters work with the Mahanta. When the unfoldment of Souls speeds up, they set the clock to the new rate.

When the unfoldment of Souls speeds up, these ECK Masters set the clock to the new rate.

A lot of cleansing is in the works today on earth. These are flush times for more people than ever, meaning the social issue of poverty is on the wane in developed countries. (But poverty abounds in other places.)

These flush times are the setup for a big fall. People believe the illusion that something can be had for almost nothing: little money, time, or effort. The hour of reckoning is near, so the Masters were adjusting the hands of time. For your part, though, love and trust the Spirit of God, the ECK, to lead you in the way of love, service, and kindness. All will be well with you.

How Is the Living ECK Master Chosen?

How is the Living ECK Master chosen, and has the next one been chosen yet?

Sometimes candidates in training for spiritual mastership move forward spiritually, then they move backward, then they move forward again.

The Living ECK Master is chosen always by God. (In ECK we call God *Sugmad.*) And there is a circle of candidates who are in training for the position of spiritual mastership.

Sometimes they move forward spiritually, then they move backward, then they move forward again. This process can go on for years until the final moment when the successor to me is chosen. At that point, God chooses the person, and I will tell others who this person is. I will tell them one way or another, either personally or by written record.

How Did the Mahanta Start?

How did the Mahanta start?

You ask a very good question. Many other ECKists would like to refresh themselves on this point too.

The three aspects of the Sugmad are the three bodies of the Mahanta: the eternal, the ECK, and the historical. The eternal Mahanta is the clear

Voice of God; it is not of time and space. The ECK: It gives life to all things. The historical Mahanta is the Living ECK Master. His deeds are recorded in history. He is the bodily manifestation of the Sugmad, the one whom people can see and talk to, the Mahanta, the Living ECK Master. He has the same qualities of the Sugmad in Its second aspect.

The historical Mahanta is the Living ECK Master. The eternal Mahanta is timeless.

Now to your question: How did the Mahanta start? The answer is in Book One of *The Shariyat-Ki-Sugmad*. It may raise other questions for those who contemplate on the words I'll quote for you:

"During the present Kali-Yuga age, the dark age, all humanity has become tormented by the thousand ills of poverty, disease, plagues, and wars instigated by jealousy, which remove man from the path of Truth. Seeing that this had happened in the worlds of the lower path, the Sugmad was moved to incarnate Itself as the Mahanta, the Living ECK Master and to give the truth of the path of salvation in simple language."

So the short answer is that the Sugmad first incarnated Itself as the Mahanta, the Living ECK Master in the *present* Kali Yuga.

"Present" refers to this lesser cycle.

The eternal Mahanta, to sum up, is timeless. But the historical Mahanta started in the present Kali Yuga.

Blending of Inner and Outer Worlds

Is the Mahanta Consciousness always with you?

It's like this: I am the Mahanta. I am the Inner Master and I am the Outer Master. Let's state this question another way: to say, Is the Mahanta Consciousness always with me? is like saying Is the outer consciousness always with me? Yes, it becomes a part of you, that you are not just the Mahanta Consciousness.

In this case, I'm saying about myself, "I'm not just the consciousness" as if it's something apart from me. I am the Mahanta because this is the blending of the inner and the outer worlds in physical form.

The Order of Mahantas

In The Golden Heart *mention is made of the Order of the Mahantas. Would you tell us more about this, please?*

It is a loosely knit brotherhood of all who once served as the Mahanta, the Living ECK Master. Their experiences were unique to that position.

Yet for all that, they do not hold themselves above or apart from other Souls, whether angel, human, animal, plant, or mineral. The members of this order exist to serve life. They obey Sugmad's bidding. This spiritual service to all living things is the reason for their being, and they would have it no other way.

They do not hold themselves above or apart from other Souls. Spiritual service to all living things is the reason for their being.

What Is Sugmad?

I have been thinking a lot these days about the Sugmad. What is It? A puzzling and perplexing subject. The mind blows up when it gets to a certain point. I think we exist in a system, and our system is tied into other systems, and so on—the worlds beyond Sugmad, as Paul Twitchell said in The Spiritual Notebook. *You have also hinted at something like this a few times. This is all my mind can handle at the moment, but it does make sense to me. A Sugmad system working within other Sugmad systems, and the supreme deity being all of those.*

So am I off base, hot, warm, or cold?

I think some Mormons, and Dr. Newton in *The Journey of Souls*, believe in a system of gods too. The ultimate world of Sugmad is above that of the minor gods. In the Ocean of Love and Mercy there are no systems or layers of anything, because that is only a space-time concept. Nor is Sugmad a deity in the popular sense of someone who watches out for us, even to seeing a sparrow fall. Most things attributed to an intervening god are done by one of those minor gods. In Eckankar, it is the ECK that intervenes or makes changes in daily life. It does that as the Voice of God—but that's not God.

It is the ECK that intervenes or makes changes in daily life. It does that as the Voice of God.

Sometimes I use rather loose terminology in my public talks in regard to what are the actions of Sugmad (if indeed there are any beyond the creation of Souls) and what are those of Its Voice, the ECK. Especially with new people in the audience. They need a language to connect the ECK teachings to something of familiarity to them. Like a personal God.

No, in the highest sense, there is no system of gods that all together constitute the Sugmad or the equivalent. Such a collection of parts is still a lower-world phenomenon.

Is the Mahanta God?

Is the Mahanta God?

You ask a very good question. In light of the fact that the Mahanta, the Living ECK Master is the

Godman, some would say yes. Others, however, are right in saying that God is God and that no Soul in the human flesh, or in any other form, can be the God of all except the Sugmad. And so it is.

In this, the ECK teachings agree with the Old Testament commandment: "Thou shalt have no other gods before me."

The Mahanta, the Living ECK Master is the Godman because he has the highest state of consciousness among all mankind. He is not God. However, he is the ECK, the Spirit, or Voice, of Sugmad. This means that the full force of the Rod of ECK Power and the Mantle of the Mahanta are embodied right in him.

So the ECK, or the Word, appears in the Master. It reveals Itself only to those whom he may choose to accept as ECK initiates. These blessed are the chosen people.

Do you see?

The ECK Energy

I want to know how the Mahanta can become the ECK Itself. Is the ECK a spiritual energy similar to bioelectric energy?

We can, of course, think of the ECK (Holy Spirit) as a spiritual energy. Yet It is that and a whole lot more. It's the very Voice of Sugmad (God), the Creative Voice that issues from the Divine Speaker.

The ECK is like a mighty river. It nourishes all life.

The ECK is like a mighty river. It nourishes all life. So everything depends upon It for existence. That's because everything *is* of It.

Bioelectric energy is a far more fundamental form of this Voice of God that our human instruments can measure in plants and animals. It is a product of the God energy, which is stepped down and down. Then It's in a form we can use. It's gone through a divine transformer.

Now, what of the Mahanta himself?

The main difference between him and all else is that he *is* the ECK. He is the God power Itself.

How, then, did he become the ECK?

It happened when he accepted the Rod of ECK Power at midnight on October 22, 1981. Sugmad had appointed him. All the power of the Holy Spirit flowed into him.

The Mahanta, the Living ECK Master is life itself. He has the ability to release people from the chains of karma and lift them into the higher worlds of God.

Co-workers with God

Who is the Mahanta's Mahanta (or what)? Do you have an ECK Master whom you identify with, or is it just the pure divine Sugmad? If so, do other ECK Masters confide in you, or do they have their own link with the Sugmad?

The Mahanta and the ECK Masters only give obeisance to the Sugmad (God). They are *Co-workers* with God.

"Co-workers" means they work with each other in love and harmony on certain missions because they want to. I have a special affinity for Peddar Zaskq (Paul Twitchell's spiritual name) and the Tibetan ECK Master Rebazar Tarzs, among others, because of their spiritual role in my life. That was during my own quest for ECK Mastership.

We enjoy each other's company the few times our duties allow us to come together. Our love is founded upon the Sugmad's love for us.

"Co-workers" means the ECK Masters work with each other in love and harmony on certain missions because they want to.

Talking about the Mahanta

How can I explain the Mahanta to my peers?

First, try to determine the level of awareness of the listeners. Do they have a most general, offhand sort of curiosity? Then say the Mahanta's like a teacher or a coach. He tries to show how to live a better life—even as a pastor, priest, or rabbi would.

Such an answer often satisfies a general curiosity.

If a questioner persists, throw questions back at him on this order: "What religion do you follow?" "How does your pastor (or priest or rabbi) try to uplift his church members?"

Listen carefully to the answer. In most cases, you can say, "My spiritual guide does that too."

Let's say that someone looks sincere and is ahead of the others in understanding. To his question you could reply, "We can talk more about that later if you like."

Above all, avoid getting into a back and forth discussion like "My spiritual guide is better than yours."

A fitting reminder to close a general discussion is to say, "God provides many religions and teachers so that everyone can choose a path that best fits his spiritual needs."

Your peers are seekers too, although unconscious of their own desire for spiritual freedom. So, say only what the situation requires, then change the subject if at all possible. And remember, I am always there beside you.

The Individual and
the Mahanta Consciousness

I hear ECKists, even High Initiates, say things like, "The Mahanta is just another word for your highest self. We are all the Mahanta." I feel uncomfortable whenever I hear this.

To me, the Mahanta is indeed the Inner Master, the teaching and uplifting aspect of the ECK, and it is a high state of consciousness. But it also involves specific responsibilities and powers, the scope of which I can only begin to imagine. I understand that you, as the Living ECK Master, have access to this state, because of your initiation level. But do others also have access to it, while you hold the Rod of ECK Power?

Could you please clarify this aspect of the relationship between the individual and the Mahanta Consciousness?

Each person relates to the ECK at his respective level of initiation.

For example, a Fourth Initiate will tap into the ECK at the level of the Fourth Circle; the wisdom of the Fifth Circle remains a mystery to him.

Each person relates to the ECK at his respective level of initiation.

Birth of the Mahanta

With permission from Eckankar, we are working on the translation of The Shariyat-Ki-Sugmad, *Book One, into Spanish. Could you please explain what the following passage means, and why it is included in* The Shariyat?

"The Mahanta is always born near or on a large body of water. His birth is always mysterious, and men of ordinary birth do not know his origin. Nor

does any man know who his sires might be, their true names, or their true origin.

"*The ECK enters into the womb of a virgin, the queen of heaven, who has submitted to the true spirit of the universe. The consciousness of the Mahanta state is planted as the seed and carefully nurtured in the womb. When the embodiment of flesh is brought into this world, a man-child is born.*"

The Mahanta's is often a life of hardship, one that sorely tests his sensitive nature.

Space is tight. Try to catch the spirit of my answer.

The Mahanta *is* always born near a large body of water—for that area. Peddar Zaskq, for example, was born near the Mississippi River—in his previous lifetime.

This lifetime? In Kentucky, a good distance from the Mississippi (itself much smaller than the Pacific Ocean).

His birth is always mysterious in spite of an ordinary human parentage, to all appearances. But he is different from his siblings. In manner he differs, and perhaps appearance, also education—which may be in abundance or paucity, or vary—and experience. He is, however, different in a very significant way. His is often a life of hardship, one that sorely tests his sensitive nature.

The "virgin," too, must be understood aright. Paul Twitchell was not the firstborn in the family, so his mother wasn't a traditional virgin. But at conception, in the rapture of love, perhaps, she did submit "to the true spirit of the universe."

St. Augustine, of the early Christian church, tried to forestall the conflict already in place between those who interpreted the Bible in a hard-and-fast literal way and those who applied common sense to obscure text.

He stressed that biblical translations do have to be accurate. But the interpretation of some passages are to be in light of the best knowledge available then to the general culture of the Christian era. St. Augustine pointed to a sticky issue about creation. The Bible says the sun, moon, and stars were made on the third day. What signaled "days" one and two, since the sun wasn't created yet?

He concluded that the "days" were periods of time, not twenty-four hours each. In the end, God made all creation's potential in the blink of an eye. See? We also use such common sense.

Simha

Sri Harold, could you tell us more about Simha, the Lady of ECK? Where does she stand in the spiritual hierarchy of the Sugmad? What would be her specific role in this hierarchy and in the development of our spiritual maturity?

Little is known about Simha, because that is her preference. She is considered to be the mother of all ECK Masters born in the world of matter. While she is not their actual mother, of course, her compassion and understanding is of great support to candidates for ECK Mastership.

Many other ECK Masters predate her. For example, Agnotti. He served as the Mahanta, the Living ECK Master during the development of primitive man. So Simha wasn't his physical mother. She came much later.

The Souls who enter the higher-consciousness realm have a choice before that lifetime. They may be either a man or a woman. In less socially developed ages, they often came to earth to serve in the

Simha's compassion and understanding is of great support to candidates for ECK Mastership.

male body because of its suitability for surviving in harsh societies. It's the reason few early Souls came back here to serve as women.

Simha, like all other ECK Masters, is not part of the male-female antagonisms bred by some cultures. She regards every individual as Soul, a light of God.

Simha regards every individual as Soul, a light of God.

So politically correct or incorrect thought or speech is not in her makeup.

She regards the cults of feminism and other aberrations like male dominance as the effects of emotional waves that cover the skies of human doings like clouds. Those under the spell of such psychic waves, she knows, is simply the response of adolescent spiritual beings whose focus is vanity.

By way of example, then, she is the very essence of humility.

A number of ECK initiates have had the grace of her spiritual instruction in the dream state.

Vairagi Adepts

On page 87 of The Shariyat-Ki-Sugmad, *Book Two, it says, "The ECK Masters, along with yet higher entities, form an inner, esoteric ring. In Eckankar they are known as the Adepts of the Vairagi." Who are the "yet higher entities"?*

You've spotted one of the more arcane areas of the ECK teachings.

There are indeed "yet higher entities" among the Adepts of the Vairagi Order. But the Mahanta, the Living ECK Master answers directly to the Sugmad for the responsibilities entrusted to him, because the Sugmad charged them to him directly.

Of the brotherhoods known at this time, there

is the Vairagi Order and a very mysterious one we know as the Nine Silent Ones. Both also answer to Sugmad alone. There's also a large body of Silent Ones made up of the Mahavakyis and the Volapuks. They run the clockworks of the spirito-material worlds and come and go like shadows.

The "yet higher entities" refers to the Council of the Nine. They are the close-knit brotherhood that took the ECK teachings underground during the time of Gopal Das. He was the Mahanta, the Living ECK Master in the early Egyptian period around 3000 BC.

It was so done because of intense persecution of all who were in ECK.

These Masters, too, answer directly to Sugmad, these unknown ones. Among their duties is to act as guardians of the ECK teachings and the distribution of ECK in the lower worlds.

A more complete revelation about these ECK orders is unavailable. It would carry no meaning for any but those of the Twelfth Circle and beyond.

But rest assured that they are all in perfect agreement with each other.

Kata Daki

There is little in the ECK works about female ECK Masters. As a female ECKist striving for mastership, I am curious about the contrasts and comparisons between female and male ECK Masters. Are they a part of the Vairagi Order? What are their roles?

Kata Daki, like all the ECK Masters, is willing to serve Sugmad (God) away from the limelight. She, too, is beyond the lure of public worship.

By all appearances, people guess her age to be

Kata Daki, like all the ECK Masters, is willing to serve Sugmad (God) away from the limelight.

from the midtwenties to early thirties, although her true age is beyond belief. Her height is five and a half feet. Light brown hair (some call it honey blond) often falls to her shoulders. But she changes hairstyles to suit her duties.

Her face catches the eye. It reflects a strong character, as do the faces of all ECK Masters.

These members of the Vairagi Order, male and female alike, are not into the games people play— like joining social or political causes. They won't limit their freedom or potential with false concepts like "victim of a glass ceiling."

They all find joy and fulfillment helping others find the Mahanta, the Living ECK Master. He holds the key to spiritual freedom.

Their roles? They all find joy, satisfaction, and fulfillment by helping others find the Mahanta, the Living ECK Master. He holds the key to spiritual freedom.

ECK Master's Training

How is someone chosen to be the new Living ECK Master? And how do you know when it's the right time? Who chooses him, and how can you be sure?

How did a cow and her calf find each other when separated in a herd in the Old West? Easy. They were of one heart and understood a private means of communication they alone shared.

So is it between the Master and each of you.

It is even more true of chelas (spiritual students) who are spiritually ready to prepare for a chance to move closer to, or into, the circle of special Souls in training for ECK Mastership.

The way is long and hard.

A candidate is always chosen by God, the Sugmad. And since the Mahanta, the Living ECK Master and all the ECK Masters, for that matter, have God

Consciousness, they know who is in tune with that First Principle.

The choice of each new Living ECK Master originates at the very top of the spiritual hierarchy—the Sugmad.

Unlike a democratic type of government, there is no popular vote. That's a good thing, too, in light of the all-too-human leadership that people choose to represent them. A spiritual Master of the ECK Order of the Vairagi Adepts, you understand, is held to a standard far above that of political or ordinary human leaders.

The Christian Bible tells how to recognize righteous people. It says, "By their fruits ye shall know them."

A commitment to walk the talk and keep on the high road to God is a most difficult one. Someone with a great love for God must also have the discipline and *courage* to go in outer and inner places where those of lesser spiritual unfoldment would pale and flee.

What distinguishes the seeker? Rebazar Tarzs, a Tibetan ECK Master, tells Peddar Zaskq, his chela, it's *purity of character and ideals.* Those are but two signs of a candidate for ECK Mastership.

Would others ascribe them to you?

The only law of the spiritual worlds is pure, divine love. If you want to see the Face of God, know that the experience can blind you or make you great. Do you love God enough to risk the downside?

How much love and courage do *you* have?

If there's enough of both, you will be drawn to God like a bee to a blossom.

And should you like to see the Face of God, what better book to use for your daily contemplations than *Stranger by the River* by Paul Twitchell?

How much love and courage do you have? If there's enough of both, you will be drawn to God like a bee to a blossom.

Fall from Grace

We hear about Darwin Gross, who was once an ECK Master. Who was he, and what did he do?

There is a spiritual explanation in the ECK writings from around the early to mid 1980s.

In short, it is a situation where an ECK Master fell from grace. History here holds a valuable spiritual lesson. Once anyone puts their feet on the path to God, they must keep their spiritual focus upon Sugmad, our name for God, the Creator.

Look through *Soul Travelers of the Far Country*; *The Living Word*, Book 1; and the Mahanta Transcripts series of books around 1983 and 1984. There you will get a sense of the spiritual conflict that once threatened the very foundation of today's reappearance of the ECK teachings.

Consciousness Nine

In one of the ECK books, it talks about your mission to bring Eckankar up to Consciousness Nine. Is this close to happening? What changes in the world could we expect to see happening as a result? What would be some changes in Eckankar?

The human race as a whole is having a time of it coming to grips with its emotions. That is Consciousness Two.

Before Paul Twitchell left this earthly theater in 1971, he set the stage for Consciousness Five, a high standard at the dividing line between the material and pure spiritual worlds. That's the general area of the consciousness of the body of ECK today.

It is trying to move into the level of Consciousness

Six—and become established there. That means no falling back.

Consciousness Six is, of course, a preliminary and necessary step of the overall spiritual level of Souls in ECK—as a body—on their way eventually to Consciousness Nine. Bear in mind that the body of ECK Souls includes life on all planes, in all universes.

My mission is to establish Consciousness Nine. I'm laying the foundation for it. The result is the social, political, economic, and climatic changes of today.

Each level is a turn higher on the spiral of consciousness, as the waves of Souls in ECK catch the returning tide home to the center of God's love, compassion, and, yes—mercy. All is of, and for, that divine love.

As Above, So Below

What plane is the Temple of Golden Wisdom of the creative arts on? Who is the guardian?

There is no one plane for such a temple.

Remember the old saying "As above, so below"? If such a temple exists on the Astral Plane, it is because its prototype already occupies the Causal Plane. The temple on the Causal Plane exists because of one already on the next-higher plane, the Mental. And so on.

The creative powers of Soul always lie with the individual.

The creative powers of Soul always lie with the individual. People with an interest in the same outlet of creative expression—like music, art, or even business—might form a group to develop that interest.

And, yes, such groups do exist here and on the higher spiritual planes. An ECK Master might even be in charge of the place where they meet. Though not always, nor as a regular thing.

Bridge to ECK

How can we use the public's interest in angels as a bridge to the ECK teachings?

Talk about the ECK Masters in the role of angels.

Entering the Eighth Circle

Please tell us more about the love, grace, and wisdom needed in order to enter the Eighth Circle of initiation, so that we can continue growing in our purity of divine service to God.

The key to the Eighth Initiation lies, of course, in the Seventh. Let's see what *The Shariyat-Ki-Sugmad*, Book Two, has to say about the Seventh:

> It is here that the initiate begins to attain direct, conscious experience. This is something which the intellectual senses cannot give him. This type of experience is concerned not with words and concepts, but with the unexplainable spiritual senses. The initiate has learned that by self-surrender he does not resist life, but goes along with it in an active manner. . . . In his relationship with the Mahanta, the Living ECK Master he accepts all the burdens of life because they will be destroyed by their own weight.

The initiate does not resist life, but goes along with it in an active manner.

These words lay the foundation for entry into the Eighth Initiation. They will help your understanding.

True Mastery

How does ECK Mastership compare to self-mastership?

True mastery is the ECK Mastership. Self-mastership can, and does, occur at earlier stages. For example, one stage on the ECK path is the Pinda Master, an individual who works in full consciousness with all the conflicting forces of the physical world. The next level of self-mastery is on the Astral Plane (emotions), and so on up to the state of ECK Mastership.

Nine Unknown Gods of Eternity

A question came up in our class on The Shariyat-Ki-Sugmad, *Book One. In chapter 4, "The Kingdom of the Sugmad," a paragraph on page 79 talks about the nine unknown Gods of Eternity, keepers of the Divine Flame of Wisdom.*

Could you tell us a little more about this paragraph? Why are they called Gods? What is the Divine Flame of Wisdom?

This is a little hard to put into words. They are called Gods because of the creative power (from the ECK) they employ to gather the sacred knowledge that derives from the unfoldment of spiritual consciousness on every plane throughout all creation. They gather it.

It's called the "Divine Flame" because they're dealing with the living truth of Sugmad Itself as It is in Its creative, living, and original form. They then transform this truth of Sugmad into knowledge.

The ECK Masters teach the divine knowledge of this truth, which is simply the manifestation of Sugmad's love, to those seekers who are ready for it. When this knowledge comes to an open heart, the result is love, wisdom, and spiritual freedom.

The ECK Masters teach the divine knowledge to those seekers who are ready for it.

Importance of Satsangs

I read in The Shariyat-Ki-Sugmad, *Book 1, "As a collective body the Satsang brings harmony, peace, and happiness to the individual, and to all entities within the universes of God."*

Please, could you remind us about the importance of Satsang, not only to the chela as an individual but to the world as a whole?

Truth is caught, not taught.

The irony is that life's lessons do demonstrate this principle, though in an untested way.

ECK Satsang classes offer a window to the Higher Self.

So encourage attendance at the ECK Satsang classes, for they offer a window to the Higher Self. The human mind needs instruction. The ECK Satsang classes teach the basic materials needed to build an individual's direct road to the highest worlds of being.

The basis for instruction in the ECK Satsang classes must always be to keep the trinity of Eckankar in the foreground.

"The trinity of Eckankar is the following:" says *The Shariyat*, Book Two, "(1) The Sat Guru, the Mahanta, the Living ECK Master; (2) the ECK Satsang, or his company of followers; and (3) the ECK, or the true name which is the Bani, or the Sound Current."

It adds: "Whenever there is a desire to develop spiritual awakening in order to attain the goal of God, one should yield to it."

World history has enjoyed the benefits of the ECK Masters' aid over the ages. They taught primitive man how to survive in a hostile environment by passing along methods of hunting and self-defense, the skills of early farming, and places and means to find dress and shelter.

For all that, those benefits are not the objective.

Once again, *The Shariyat*, Book Two, says: "But anything other than giving the human race an uplift of spiritual value has never been the aim of the ECK Masters."

It's been to help mankind reach perfection through the Spiritual Exercises of ECK.

The Master's Satsang

Do you go to Satsang? If you do, what do you do in it? Can you tell me a little bit about you?

You ask a good question I've not been asked before.

Yes, I do—I teach it.

Much of my instruction occurs on the inner and outer planes to *groups*, but also one on one. You probably never thought of this, yet my talks at ECK seminars are Satsang. You, other chelas (spiritual students), and I are in company with each other. That is Satsang.

Some of my outer teaching and demonstration of the ECK (Holy Spirit) takes place with *individuals*. This means chelas and non-chelas. These "chance" meetings occur in stores, at the post office, on the street, in shopping malls, and in other places. Each who meets the Living ECK Master on the inner or outer planes has earned the right.

It is a special privilege.

On every occasion I love such meetings, because the ECK has set the time and place for it. Its will is my will.

Do you know the meaning of "Satsang"? It means

Each who meets the Living ECK Master on the inner or outer planes has earned the right.

true union. Then, one is in the company of the Living ECK Master or one of the Higher Initiates. So you are likely to be in Satsang more than you know.

And you wanted to hear a little more about me.

In my public meetings with non-ECKists, the ECK teachings never come up. We simply enjoy a conversation about everyday things. In time, they'll be ready for ECK. Nobody need be in a hurry.

Nobody need be in a hurry.

About the Author

Author Harold Klemp is known as a pioneer of today's focus on "everyday spirituality." He was raised on a Wisconsin farm and attended divinity school. He also served in the U.S. Air Force.

In 1981, after years of training, he became the spiritual leader of Eckankar, Religion of the Light and Sound of God.

His full title is Sri Harold Klemp, the Mahanta, the Living ECK Master. His mission is to help people find their way back to God in this life.

Each year, Harold Klemp speaks to thousands of seekers at Eckankar seminars. Author of more than sixty books, he continues to write, including many articles and spiritual-study discourses. His inspiring and practical approach to spirituality helps thousands of people worldwide find greater freedom, wisdom, and love in their lives.

Next Steps in Spiritual Exploration

- **Try a spiritual exercise** on a daily basis.
  Review the spiritual exercises in this book. Experiment with them.

- **Browse our Web site: www.Eckankar.org**
  Watch videos; get free books, answers to FAQs, and more info.

- **Attend an Eckankar event** in your area.
  Visit "Eckankar around the World" on our Web site.

- **Explore an advanced spiritual study class**
  (or study privately) with the Eckankar discourses that come with membership.

- **Read additional books** about the ECK teachings.

Advanced Spiritual Study

Advanced spiritual study is available through yearly membership in Eckankar. This annual cycle of study and practice focuses on the ECK discourses, which may be studied privately or in a class. Each year the spiritual student decides whether to continue with his or her studies in Eckankar.

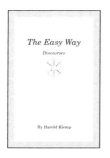

Discourses

As you study the teachings of ECK, you will find a series of changes in your heart and mind that can make you a better, stronger, and more happy person.

Each month of the year, you'll study a new discourse lesson and practice a new technique to enhance your spiritual journey.

The twelve lessons in *The Easy Way*

Discourses by Harold Klemp include these titles and more: "In Soul You Are Free," "Dream On, Sweet Dreamer," "Reincarnation—Why You Came to Earth Again," "The Master Principle," and "The God Worlds—Where No One Has Gone Before?"

Books

If you would like to read additional books by Harold Klemp about the ECK teachings, you may find these of special interest. They are available at bookstores, online booksellers, or directly from Eckankar.

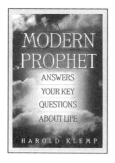

A Modern Prophet Answers Your Key Questions about Life, Book 1

A pioneer of today's focus on "everyday spirituality" shows you how to experience and understand God's love in your life—anytime, anyplace. His answers to hundreds of questions help guide you to your own source of wisdom, peace, and deep inner joy.

The Call of Soul

Harold Klemp takes you on an amazing journey into a world you may only dare to dream of—the infinite world of God's love for you. More, he shows, through spiritual exercises, dream techniques, and Soul Travel explorations, how this love translates into every event, relationship, and moment of your life. Includes a CD with dream and Soul Travel techniques.

HU, the Most Beautiful Prayer

The simple spiritual exercises in this book will open your heart to see God's loving presence in your life. Includes a CD with the sound of thousands of people singing this powerful, majestic love song to God. Read about HU or listen or sing along with the recording. Singing HU can lift you spiritually, no matter your age, background, or religion.

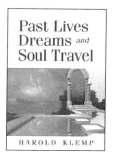

Past Lives, Dreams, and Soul Travel

These stories and exercises help you find your true purpose, discover greater love than you've ever known, and learn that spiritual freedom is within reach.

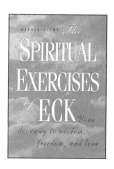

The Spiritual Exercises of ECK

This book is a staircase with 131 steps leading to the doorway to spiritual freedom, self-mastery, wisdom, and love. A comprehensive volume of spiritual exercises for every need.

How to Survive Spiritually in Our Times, Mahanta Transcripts, Book 16

Discover how to reinvent yourself spiritually—to thrive in a changing world. Stories, tools, techniques, and spiritual insights to apply in your life now.

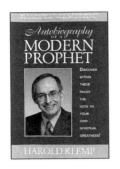

Autobiography of a Modern Prophet

This riveting story of Harold Klemp's climb up the Mountain of God will help you discover the keys to your own spiritual greatness.

Those Wonderful ECK Masters

Would you like to have *personal* experience with spiritual masters that people all over the world—since the beginning of time—have looked to for guidance, protection, and divine love? This book includes real-life stories and spiritual exercises to meet eleven ECK Masters.

The Spiritual Laws of Life

Learn how to keep in tune with your true spiritual nature. Spiritual laws reveal the behind-the-scenes forces at work in your daily life.

How to Get Started

To request information about ECK books or to sign up for ECK membership and get your advanced spiritual study discourses along with other membership benefits (renewable annually), you may:

- Join online at "Membership" at www.Eckankar.org (click on "Online Membership Application"), or

- Call Eckankar (952) 380-2222 to apply, or

- Write to:
  ECKANKAR, Att: Information, BK 91
  PO Box 2000
  Chanhassen, MN 55317-2000 USA

Glossary

Words set in SMALL CAPS are defined elsewhere in this glossary.

Arahata. *ah-rah-HAH-tah* An experienced and qualified teacher of ECKANKAR classes.

Blue Light. How the MAHANTA often appears in the inner worlds to the CHELA or seeker.

chela. *CHEE-lah* A spiritual student. Often refers to a member of ECKANKAR.

ECK. *EHK* The Life Force, the Holy Spirit, or Audible Life Current which sustains all life.

Eckankar. *EHK-ahn-kahr* Religion of the Light and Sound of God. Also known as the Ancient Science of SOUL TRAVEL. A truly spiritual religion for the individual in modern times. The teachings provide a framework for anyone to explore their own spiritual experiences. Established by PAUL TWITCHELL, the modern-day founder, in 1965. The word means "Co-worker with God."

ECK Master(s). Spiritual Masters who can assist and protect people in their spiritual studies and travels. The ECK Masters are from a long line of God-Realized SOULS who know the responsibility that goes with spiritual freedom.

ECK Rite of Passage. One of the Four ECK Celebrations of Life. This ceremony is for youth on the threshold of becoming adults, at about age thirteen. It celebrates a personal commitment to the ECK teachings, to accepting the presence of the MAHANTA, and to becoming more aware of one's true spiritual nature.

Fubbi Quantz. *FOO-bee KWAHNTS* The guardian of the SHARIYAT-KI-SUGMAD at the Katsupari Monastery in northern Tibet. He was the MAHANTA, the LIVING ECK MASTER during the time of Buddha, about 500 BC.

God-Realization.   The state of God Consciousness. Complete and conscious awareness of God.

Gopal Das. *GOH-pahl DAHS*   The guardian of the SHARIYAT-KI-SUGMAD at the Temple of Askleposis on the Astral PLANE. He was the MAHANTA, the LIVING ECK MASTER in Egypt, about 3000 BC.

HU. *HYOO*   The most ancient, secret name for God. The singing of the word *HU* is considered a love song to God. It can be sung aloud or silently to oneself.

initiation.   Earned by a member of ECKANKAR through spiritual unfoldment and service to God. The initiation is a private ceremony in which the individual is linked to the Sound and Light of God.

Kal Niranjan, the. *KAL nee-RAHN-jahn*   The Kal; the negative power, also known as Satan or the devil.

Karma, Law of.   The Law of Cause and Effect, action and reaction, justice, retribution, and reward, which applies to the lower or psychic worlds: the Physical, Astral, Causal, Mental, and Etheric PLANES.

Kata Daki. *KAH-tah DAH-kee*   A female ECK MASTER, who, like all others in the Order of the Vairagi, serves the SUGMAD by helping others find the MAHANTA, the LIVING ECK MASTER. Her pet project is to help people get back on their feet during hardship.

Klemp, Harold.   The present MAHANTA, the LIVING ECK MASTER. SRI Harold Klemp became the Mahanta, the Living ECK Master in 1981. His spiritual name is WAH Z.

Lai Tsi. *lie TSEE*   An ancient Chinese ECK MASTER.

Living ECK Master.   The title of the spiritual leader of ECKANKAR. His duty is to lead SOUL back to God. The Living ECK Master can assist spiritual students physically as the Outer Master, in the dream state as the Dream Master, and in the spiritual worlds as the Inner Master. SRI HAROLD KLEMP became the MAHANTA, the Living ECK Master in 1981.

Mahanta. *mah-HAHN-tah*   A title to describe the highest state of God Consciousness on earth, often embodied in the LIVING ECK MASTER. He is the Living Word. An expression of the Spirit of God that is always with you. Sometimes seen as a BLUE LIGHT or Blue Star or in the form of the Mahanta, the Living ECK Master.

Mahdis. *MAH-dees*   The initiate of the Fifth Circle (SOUL PLANE); often used as a generic term for all High Initiates in ECK.

Peddar Zaskq. *PEH-dahr ZASK*   The spiritual name for PAUL TWITCHELL, the modern-day founder of ECKANKAR and the MAHANTA, the LIVING ECK MASTER from 1965 to 1971.

plane(s).   The levels of existence, such as the Physical, Astral, Causal, Mental, Etheric, and SOUL planes.

Rami Nuri. *RAH-mee NOO-ree*   The guardian of the SHARIYAT-KI-SUGMAD at the House of Moksha in the city of Retz, Venus. He served as the MAHANTA, the LIVING ECK MASTER. The letter *M* appears on his forehead.

Rebazar Tarzs. *REE-bah-zahr TAHRZ*   A Tibetan ECK MASTER known as the Torchbearer of ECKANKAR in the lower worlds.

Satsang. *SAHT-sahng*   A class in which students of ECK study a monthly lesson from ECKANKAR.

Self-Realization. SOUL recognition.   The entering of Soul into the Soul PLANE and there beholding Itself as pure Spirit. A state of seeing, knowing, and being.

Shariyat-Ki-Sugmad. *SHAH-ree-aht-kee-SOOG-mahd*   The sacred scriptures of ECKANKAR. The scriptures are comprised of about twelve volumes in the spiritual worlds. The first two were transcribed from the inner PLANES by PAUL TWITCHELL, modern-day founder of Eckankar.

Soul.   The True Self. The inner, most sacred part of each person. Soul exists before birth and lives on after the death of the physical body. As a spark of God, Soul can see, know, and perceive all things. It is the creative center of Its own world.

Soul Travel.   The expansion of consciousness. The ability of SOUL to transcend the physical body and travel into the spiritual worlds of God. Soul Travel is taught only by the LIVING ECK MASTER. It helps people unfold spiritually and can provide proof of the existence of God and life after death.

Sound and Light of ECK.   The Holy Spirit. The two aspects through which God appears in the lower worlds. People can experience them by looking and listening within themselves and through SOUL TRAVEL.

Spiritual Exercises of ECK.   The daily practice of certain techniques to get us in touch with the Light and Sound of God.

Sri. *SREE*   A title of spiritual respect, similar to reverend or pastor, used for those who have attained the Kingdom of God. In ECKANKAR, it is reserved for the MAHANTA, the LIVING ECK MASTER.

Sugmad. *SOOG-mahd*   A sacred name for God. Sugmad is neither masculine nor feminine; It is the source of all life.

Temple(s) of Golden Wisdom.   These Golden Wisdom Temples are spiritual temples which exist on the various PLANES—from the Physical to the Anami Lok; CHELAS of ECKANKAR are taken to the temples in the SOUL body to be educated in the divine knowledge; the different sections of the SHARIYAT-KI-SUGMAD, the sacred teachings of ECK, are kept at these temples.

Twitchell, Paul.   An American ECK MASTER who brought the modern teachings of ECKANKAR to the world through his writings and lectures. His spiritual name is PEDDAR ZASKQ.

Vahana. *vah-HAH-nah*   Vehicle; carrier of ECK or the message of ECK; the ECK missionary.

vairag. *vie-RAHG*   Detachment.

Wah Z. *WAH zee*   The spiritual name of SRI HAROLD KLEMP. It means the secret doctrine. It is his name in the spiritual worlds.

Yaubl Sacabi. *YEEOW-buhl sah-KAH-bee*   Guardian of the SHARIYAT-KI-SUGMAD in the spiritual city of Agam Des. He was the MAHANTA, the LIVING ECK MASTER in ancient Greece.

For more explanations of ECKANKAR terms, see *A Cosmic Sea of Words: The ECKANKAR Lexicon* by Harold Klemp.